Michael Nodde

Ethics in Nigerian Culture

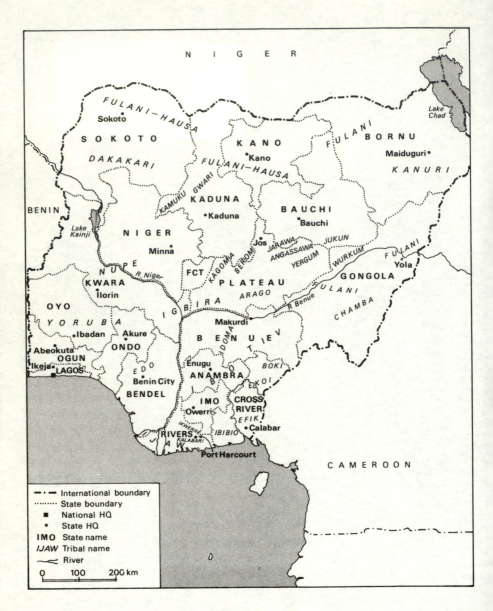

The states and major tribes of Nigeria
(Note: Hausa is not a tribe but a group of many tribes)

Ethics in Nigerian Culture

ELECHI AMADI

Heinemann Educational Books (Nigeria) Ltd
Ibadan

Heinemann Educational Books (Nigeria) Ltd
Head Office: PMB 5205, Ighodaro Road, Ibadan
Phone: 617060, 617061   Telex: 31113   Cable HEBOOKS, Ibadan

Area Offices and Branches:
Ibadan   Ikeja   Akure   Benin   Ilorin   Owerri
Enugu   Uyo   Port Harcourt   Jos   Maiduguri
Makurdi   Zaria   Kano   Minna

Heinemann Educational Books Ltd
22 Bedford Square, London WC1B 3HH

NAIROBI   EDINBURGH   MELBOURNE   AUCKLAND
SINGAPORE   HONG KONG   KUALA LUMPUR   NEW DELHI
KINGSTON   PORT OF SPAIN

Heinemann Educational Books Inc.
4 Front Street, Exeter, New Hampshire 03833, USA

ISBN 0 435 89030 1 (UK)
ISBN 978 129 596 1 (Nigeria)

British Library Cataloguing in Publication Data

Amadi, Elechi
    Ethics in Nigerian culture.
    1. Nigeria—Civilization—Moral and religious aspects.
    I. Title
    966.9   DT515.4

ISBN 0-435-89030-1

Set in 10 pt Baskerville by Willmer Brothers Limited,
Birkenhead, Merseyside
Printed and bound in Great Britain by Biddles Limited,
Guildford, Surrey

Contents

Introduction

Ethics is a difficult subject. As in many branches of philosophy, much of this difficulty arises from differences in definitions and the limitations of language itself. Although I have not hesitated to offer opinions here and there, this book is mainly descriptive and so is not concerned with definitions and ethical theories.

Yet there are immense problems associated with discussing the ethical practices of a country like Nigeria, with well over 250 tribes. One cannot hope to cover even a tenth of these exhaustively, and were such a feat possible, the result would stretch to several volumes. Again, even the most extensive field research cannot now give an accurate picture of the ethical scene beyond a century ago. (In fact, the oldest living Nigerians cannot recall events beyond 1900.)

To deal with these problems I have had to rely on three sources of information for this work. The first source is my own experience as a forty-six-year-old Nigerian who has lived all his life in Nigeria except for a few months abroad now and then. Moreover, I was lucky to have spent five years in Yoruba country (Oyo and Ibadan), three among the Hausa (Zaria and Kaduna) and five years with the Igbo (Enugu and Umuahia). For much of the rest of the time I have lived among my own tribe, the Ikwerre, who occupy the eastern rainforest belt between the Ijaw of the Niger Delta and the Igbo; but even here I have always had friends, colleagues and neighbours from all over the Federation.

My second source is the product of field work carried out through questionnaires and personal interviews with students, teachers, businessmen, villagers and ordinary men and women in various professions. It was not possible to acquire information on secret societies directly. For this I have had to rely on documents already published on the matter and on my own observations.

Published anthropological and historical accounts, especially those by colonial administrative officers and explorers, provide the third source. This source reaches furthest back in time. Amaury Talbot's *The Peoples of Southern Nigeria*, C. K. Meek's *The Northern Tribes of Nigeria* and C. L. Temple's *Notes on the Tribes of Northern Nigeria* have been particularly useful. How objective and reliable are these reports? Fortunately for me, Talbot covered my own tribe, the Ikwerre (he spells it Ikwerri), very well in his writings, and so it has been possible for me to verify some of his accounts. I consider his field reports very reliable. His interpretations are less so, and no wonder, for it is extremely difficult for anyone outside a given culture to interpret that culture accurately. Talbot himself recognized this fact when he said: 'Long sojourn in Africa should ... teach caution even to the most careless inquirer and we therefore, as always took the precaution to keep our ideas to ourselves ... .'[1] In spite of this admirable scientific caution, the temptation to generalize sometimes overcame him, as when he declared, 'Among Ibo, as with the ancient Egyptians also, the feminine, as well as the male genital organs are worshipped.'[2] This is not true. In fact, the contrary is the case. The genital organs, particularly the female organs, are often subjects of light-hearted jokes and derision among the Igbo. Such errors in interpretation notwithstanding, Talbot's work is brilliant and shows a level of objectivity unusual in colonial administrator-anthropologists who, in the circumstances then prevailing, had an understandable superiority complex. This complex showed in C. K. Meek's un-mistakable glee when he quoted Virgil's description of negro women as 'splay-footed' and 'blubber-lipped'.[3] Still, Meek was an accomplished anthropologist. A. G. Leonard is the author who was most incapacitated by this superiority complex. He wrote with little or no empathy and was prone to startling generalizations which force one to question the accuracy of his field observations in the first place. For instance, in describing Delta households he wrote: 'In a word the ordinary household is nothing but a hotbed of evil passions that, underneath an outwardly calm surface, is seething with mental visions and apparitions that readily take the form of the devouring death friend'.[4] This description can hardly fit any tribe in the world, least of all Nigerian tribes, which are noted for their very strong family ties. Any tribe with such an explosive family set-up would be destined for extinction. This kind of unguarded generalization mars Leonard's *The Lower Niger and its Tribes*. Temple's compilation comprises field reports by at least ninety-six colonial administrators and field workers. Little or no attempt is made to analyse the facts or draw far-fetched conclusions. This, in my view, increases the reliability of the reports. However, errors there are bound to be. C. L. Temple, the editor, wrote in his preface:

As is inevitable when large and heterogeneous populations have to be studied and facts gleaned *viva voce* from natives sometimes unwilling to impart information, much has been recorded as fact which is incorrect and many omissions of important facts occur. These pages necessarily reflect such errors and omissions.[5]

For proverbs which feature promimently in this work, I have had to rely largely on *Hausa, Ba Dabo Ba Ne*, compiled by A. H. M. Kirk-Green; *Owe Yoruba*, by J. O. Ajibola; and *Elulu Ikwerre*, by S. A. Ekwulo. For the rest I have had to rely on field work and on my own knowledge.

Naturally, I have made frequent reference to Ikwerre because it is the tribe I know best. I believe anyone in my place would also draw heavily from his knowledge of his own tribe. This is not necessarily a disadvantage. Indeed, it is difficult to discuss ethical values meaningfully without the experience of a deep involvement in at least one ethical system somewhere.

This book is a direct result of my interest in cultural studies which was aroused and enhanced by the effort I had to make to write three novels and a verse play, all of whose themes are confined entirely to the Nigerian culture. No special knowledge is claimed, nor are there pretensions to scholarship. Indeed, I am well aware of the limitations of my field work. This, then, is a layman's rendering of a very intricate subject. Nevertheless, a serious effort has been made to provide factual information and analysis.

It is a fact that the field of philosophy has been almost completely ignored by Nigerian intellectuals. There is a general feeling that Nigerians are too poor, too hungry and too underdeveloped to philosophize. But then philosophy has a direct effect on the pattern of thought, the politics and government of a people, and ultimately therefore on its moral, material and mental development. The reticence of Nigerian intellectuals on this subject should therefore be a cause for concern.

My thanks are due to Professor Kay Williamson and Professor E. J. Alagoa, who made their private libraries available to me; to Mr and Mrs Aig Higo, whose home at Ibadan I converted into a research centre; and to my daughters Chinyere and Nyege who worked on the index.

Elechi Amadi
Port Harcourt

Chapter 1

Religion

The villagers may belong to a god, but the god also belongs to the villagers.
(Ikwerre proverb)

Over the past two centuries man has made impressive advances in science. He can fly, cure diverse diseases, reconstruct living creatures through genetic engineering, arrest time through pictures, tapes and films, transmit his voice across vast spaces, explore nearby planets and commit mass murder of harrowing proportions in a matter of seconds. It is a long road indeed from the largely instinct-controlled ape-man to the creature that can now grasp the concepts of quantum mechanics and relativity. But he is still deplorably ignorant and the universe is largely a mystery to him. He does not understand the nature of space and time; he does not know what matter is made of, if indeed it is made of anything; above all, he does not understand himself.

Some of these puzzles are, by their very nature, impossible to unravel, and this is one of the main reasons why man resorts to religion. In his essay entitled 'Why I am not a Christian', Bertrand Russell explains religion in terms of fear. He says:

> Religion is based, I think, primarily and mainly upon fear. It is partly the terror of the unknown and partly, as I have said, the wish to feel that you have a kind of elder brother who will stand by you in all your troubles and disputes.[1]

This is a half-truth. A strong desire to explain the mysteries of the universe appears to be partly responsible for the evolution of religion. For the believer the notion of God seems to bring an end to an otherwise endless stream of questions. But it is also true that for the cynic God provides no relief, for he wants to know who made God. If we can believe that God has no beginning or end, why, he asks, can we not believe the same of matter? Russell puts it this way: 'If everything must have a cause, then God must have a cause. If there can be anything without a cause, it may just as well be the world as God.'[2] Actually, there is very little difference between belief in God and belief in matter. In the first place, both positions require blind faith and can admit of no proof. Secondly, belief in matter implies that matter has always had, and will always have, life as one of its properties. Thus wherever matter exists there will always be spontaneous generation of life if conditions are right. But life is not merely vegetative. In man life has attained that awesome level of consciousness which we normally attribute to God. If, then, we attribute the creative power to matter – and we have no choice if we discard God – it means that every bit of matter has the capacity for conscious existence when it is arranged, by natural forces, in a certain manner, as, for instance, in protein molecules. Thus the creative power is all-pervading (that is, omnipresent) and omniscient, since all knowledge depends on intelligence, intelligence on life and life on matter. Believers in God also describe him as omnipresent and omniscient. Thus God and the creative power in matter are indistinguishable: that is, God and the universe form one mysterious package, and it is futile to try to isolate one from the other. All the questions we ask about matter and the universe could be asked about God. Since most men do not doubt the existence of the universe (though some philosophers, like Berkeley, do), they have to believe in an all-powerful creative force or God. When some people say they do not believe in God, much of the time they are referring to the God which religious organizations have created in the image of man. This God has all the limitations of man. He is emotional, greedy for praise, adoration and appreciation; he punishes or rewards human beings according to the state of his mind at any particular time. Besides, most religious groups have awkward articles of faith that must be believed. If religion were divested of these elements, then perhaps the differences between science, religion and philosophy would vanish.

Unfortunately a non-human image of God is, for most people, impossible to conceptualize. A god without human attributes would seem remote, forbidding and unsympathetic. But man needs protection and sympathy, so his quasi-human gods will always stay with him. Also, the human mind, in spite of its brilliance, is quite limited. It buckles when it tries to grapple with any concept concerning the infinitely great or the infinitesimally small. Even language fails him. It may be that there is no real disagreement between believers and non-believers in God. A failure of imagination and language may well account for all the wrangling. God merely represents all that we do not know about the universe.

Clearly, then, religion has always been a very powerful factor in human life. It has inspired wars, heroism, martyrdom, and creativity. One has only to think of the Crusades, the *Jihads*, Milton's *Paradise Lost*, Michaelangelo's painting in the Sistine Chapel of St Peter's in Rome, Handel's *Messiah* or the pyramids to recognize the immense power of religious fervour.

Like every powerful weapon, religion can and has been used for good and ill. Kings have claimed divine authority as their excuse to rule their fellow men. Charles I of England, an exponent of the Divine Right of Kings, pushed the matter too far, and his countrymen were obliged to execute him. In Japan the emperor renounced his divinity only in 1947. In Nigeria the king of the Jukun is semi-divine, while many traditional rulers are priest-kings whose curses are said to be fatal to their subjects.

Religion has played a particularly important role in ethical philosophy all down the ages because it has been a useful instrument for enforcing moral codes. One should do this and not do that because God has said so. Much of the ancient and medieval philosophy of the Western world hinged on religious precepts. The medieval philosopher found God a very useful resort, the point at which all arguments ended. This is how St Augustine (354–430) accounts for the existence of evil:

> All things that exist therefore, seeing that the Creator of them all is supremely good, are themselves good. But because they are not, like their Creator, supremely and unchangeably good, their good may be diminished and increased. But for good to be diminished is an evil.[3]

Of law St Thomas Aquinas (1225–74) writes:

> In order, therefore, that man may know without any doubt what he ought to do and what he ought to avoid, it was necessary for man to be directed in his proper acts by a law given by God, for it is certain that such a law cannot err.[4]

In his book *Olodumare*, Bolaji Idowu writes without reservation:

> With the Yoruba morality is certainly the fruit of religion. They do not attempt to separate the two and it is impossible for them to do so without disastrous consequences.[5]

Russell agrees when he writes:

Many traditional ethical beliefs are hard to justify, except on the assumption that there is a God or a World Spirit or at least an immanent Cosmic Purpose.[6]

One problem was how to convince the would-be believer that a particular precept was, in fact, an order from God. This problem was solved through elaborate testimony and evidence that showed that God spoke directly to his messengers or delivered the written laws himself. The Ten Commandments transmitted to the children of Israel through Moses was God's direct law:

> And God spoke these words saying, I am the Lord thy God, which brought thee out of the land of Egypt, out of the house of bondage. Thou shalt have no other god but me. . . .[7]

The Koran which, like the Bible, is filled with moral precepts was handed over to the holy Prophet Mohammed (to whom be peace) by God. The Book of Mormon was delivered to Joseph Smith in bits, written by God himself on tablets of pure gold. Here is Joseph Smith's own account of the event:

> On the twenty-second day of September, one thousand eight hundred and twenty-seven, having gone as usual at the end of another year to the place where they were deposited, the same heavenly messenger delivered them up to me. . . .[8]

In Nigerian traditional religion the priests of Ifa, Amadioha, Chukwu and other gods still act as intermediaries between men and gods and interpret their commands, which often contain patterns of behaviour.

Even when the authority of a deity has been established through evidence of sorts, some man may ask: what if I refuse to obey the orders of a god? Religion has an answer to that: the god may intervene directly and may deal with a disobedient man by subjecting him to misfortune, illness and death. In Yoruba belief Esu, the god of discipline, punishes all those who refuse to carry out propitiatory sacrifices for their misbehaviour.[9] What is more sobering, punishment may continue in the after-life. According to the Christian religion, punishment after death means everlasting torment in Hellfire. For those who obey there is the promise of eternal life in Heaven. Life after death is one of mankind's most fascinating and abiding speculations, and few are prepared to gamble with it. In *The City of God* St Augustine writes:

> If then we be asked what ... the supreme good and evil is ... [we]
> reply that life eternal is the supreme good, death eternal the
> supreme evil, and that to obtain the one and escape the other we
> must live rightly.[10]

In Nigeria many traditional religions subscribe to the belief in some
form of life after death. Some, like the Dukawa, believe in the existence of
a heaven and a hell that are very similar to those of Christian belief.
According to Temple:

> The Dukawa believe in a future life in a place they call 'Andakka'.
> There the wicked are isolated for a term of two years, throughout
> which they have neither food nor shelter. The good are met by their
> predeceased friends, who bring them cloths and food and beer. A
> dying man will often say that he hears his friends calling to him. For
> them this is heaven.[11]

Exceptions, like the Ekiti tribe, are very few. According to Temple: 'The
Ekiti say that there is no future state, that the dead are neither reborn to
this world, nor is there another.'[12] Some Ekiti interviewed on the matter
refuted Temple's assertions. They pointed out that they have names like
Babatunde ('Father has come back') and they believe in Abiku, the child
who dies soon after birth only to be reborn again and again, causing his
mother much agony. Also Oguntuyi, in *History of Ekiti*, indicates the
belief in Abiku and life after death.[13]

Of those who believe in an after-life, a large proportion believe in
reincarnation, among them Igbo, Yoruba and many northern tribes, like
Jukun, Taba, Jarawa, Kagoro, Kagoma, Kugama, Gwari, Yergum,
Chamba, Kaje, Berom, Angab and Igara. The assertion by A. G.
Leonard that the spirits chosen for reincarnation 'are invariably those of
strong and pugnacious character or moral stamina, especially those who
had been excellent domestic managers, traders, farmers or hunters',[14] is
not true. In popular Nigerian belief incarnation is open to all, the weak
and the strong, the poor and the rich, the good and the wicked. In spite of
the differences in detail, the belief in reincarnation is very strong in
Nigeria and negates John Mbiti's assertion that 'As far as traditional
African concepts are concerned death is death and the beginning of a
permanent ontological departure of the individual from mankind to
spirithood.'[15] This conclusion may be a correct interpretation of the
concepts of traditional East African religion, but it is not true of Nigeria.

For tribes who believe in reincarnation, punishment in the after-life really means punishment in the next incarnation. In Ikwerre theology a woman who is wicked to her children in this life will be childless in her next life; a wicked rich man will be poor and miserable; a cold-blooded murderer will be helplessly deformed and so on. The Angas believe that after death the great god Nan receives the souls of all good men, while those of bad men become *kapwans*, lingering near their old homes and harassing the living.[16] The Nupe believe that evil men never attain heaven but are turned into beasts.[17]

The overall effect of all this is to enforce a moral standard acceptable to a particular society. A secular interpretation leads to the conclusion that moral precepts have always had their origin in the mind of man. Even where deities are said to have laid them down, they have had to do so through the mind of man. It would appear, then, that while man formulates the moral code, he enlists the influence of religion for its enforcement. In other words, in ethics man proposes, god enforces.

The imported religions, namely Christianity and Islam, do not have the same powerful hold on the people as the traditional religions, so their use as ethical instruments is not as effective. In this regard, Idowu observes in *Olodumare*:

> Christianity, by a miscarriage of purpose, makes its own contribution to the detrimental changes in moral values. Somehow it has replaced the old fear of the divinities with the relieving but harmful notion of a God who is ready to forgive perhaps even more than man is prone to sin, the God in whom 'goodness and severity' have been put asunder. So also does Islam unwittingly create the erroneous impression that the fulfilment of the obligatory duties and acts of penance by good works are sufficient for the purpose of winning heaven. The result of all these is that our 'enlightened' products of the two 'fashionable' religions can now steal without any twinge of moral compunction those articles of food placed for sale at cross roads and by roadsides, which used to be quite safe; they can now cheerfully appropriate other persons' property; they can break covenants, or promises made on oath, with brazen indifference.[18]

As he is an ordained minister and the current head of the Methodist Church of Nigeria, the Reverend Idowu's comments carry much weight.

There is a religious revolution going on now in Nigeria, manifested by the rise of the spiritual churches. It seems that there are three main reasons for this movement. First, it is a natural reaction against the violence suffered by traditional religion as a result of the introduction of imported religion. Second, it is a rebellion against the authority of the Christian Church, which for years has propagated forms of worship alien to the people. Third, it is a bid for power. When anyone initiates a spiritual church he automatically becomes the bishop of the new church, and his followers quickly assume the titles of apostle, prophet and the like.

Members of spiritual churches are drawn from all sections of society. It is not at all unusual for a top businessman or civil servant to be seen in the streets, clad in a white robe and ringing a huge bell, singing and dancing at the head of a religious procession. A study of these churches reveals that they seek to incorporate elements of indigenous religion into the formal Christian religion. Their mode of worship is very Nigerian. Traditional musical instruments are used instead of the organ, and the songs are very similar to those used in the shrines of local deities. Worshippers clap, sing, drum and dance, sometimes far into the night. Often members become possessed and see visions at the height of the singing and drumming. Most spiritual churches have prophets and apostles who are reputed to have the powers of traditional medicine men. They heal the sick, prophesy, divine the causes of misfortunes and prescribe sacrifices that are not very different from those normally prescribed by traditional medicine men. But at the same time they read the Bible and pray through Jesus Christ. Although adherents of these new churches are generally more devoted than those of the more formal Protestant churches, they are still not as devoted as the practitioners of traditional religion. Indeed, in times of real crisis most of them resort to traditional religion. The movement will continue until a fairly respectable and appealing hybrid religion emerges.

It is not only the spiritual churches that are trying to weld traditional concepts with imported religion. The established, orthodox churches have not been idle. In *Christianity and Igbo Culture* the Reverend Edmund Ilogu, making a case for the belief in ancestral spirits, writes pointedly: 'Our recommendation therefore is that all Ibos, Christian as well as non-Christian, acknowledge this link with our patrilineal ancestors in the pouring of libation and in the giving of pieces of kola-nut.'[19] In my view, this signals the beginning of attempts by learned Nigerian theologians to break free from the stranglehold of foreign religion and to acknowledge the beauty, wisdom and power of their own.

Chapter 2

Secret Societies

When a man acts as a traitor secretly, evil things will happen
to him secretly. (Yoruba proverb)

Many secret societies exist in Nigeria. In 1977 the Federal Military
Government, suspecting that some of these societies interferred with
administration in the civil service and with justice in the courts, decreed
that members should renounce their membership or quit public service.
The previous civilian government had banned the Owegbe cult in 1966
and had destroyed the shrine of Igwekala at Omunoha in the same year.

Secret societies usually have religious overtones. Often members are
required to swear not to reveal the activities of the society. Such oaths are
sworn by local deities powerful enough to restrain the swearer effectively
as required. In some societies the religious component is restricted to the
oaths. In others religious rites form an important aspect of the activities
of the society. Secret societies have as their aims a number of socially
important objectives. These will now be examined.

First, all secret societies endeavour to protect their members from
harm, inflicted by non-members. This protection is usually achieved
through the influence of members who are placed in privileged positions.
For instance, one fear which the Federal Military Government had was
the possibility that a High Court judge, say, might be influenced in his
judgement by his desire to protect members of his society, or that a
highly placed civil servant might favour members of his cult in the
matter of employment. Whether or not this fear was justified, there is no
doubt that members of secret societies are expected to help one another.
It is hard to tell where they draw the line.

Second, members of secret societies usually strive to gain a
psychological advantage over the rest of the population. They
deliberately create the impression that they possess esoteric knowledge
and spiritual or special powers beyond the reach of others. Their very
secrecy lends them an air of mystery. Thus the rest of the population
tends to stand in awe of them. Since the acquisition of power of some sort

is a basic and powerful human desire, secret societies are almost always irresistibly attractive to people who would otherwise feel psychologically or socially insecure.

This psychological leverage sets the stage for the third function of secret societies, which is to prescribe and to enforce laws, especially moral laws, within and outside the societies. Sometimes such laws are beneficial to society as a whole; at other times they are devised for the convenience of members of the cult only. Whatever the nature of these laws, they affect (sometimes to a considerable extent) moral behaviour in society, and this is our main concern here. An examination of some secret societies will illustrate the points discussed above.

The Ogboni society is probably the best known secret society in Nigeria. Its members are drawn from all walks of life. According to Fadipe in *The Sociology of the Yoruba*, 'The Ogboni secret society is an association found in all parts of Yoruba.'[1] Actually, nowadays members are found in practically all parts of the country. One sees photographs of members in their regalia hanging in quite a few homes in Port Harcourt and other cities outside Yoruba country. The society prescribes modes of behaviour for its members and takes an active interest in what goes on in the rest of society. According to Fadipe, 'The society could take energetic and suitable action in dealing with any threatened menace to the social and political order.'[2] In Ile-Ife the society was said to have functioned at one time as a court for dealing with chiefs.

Apart from its more serious functions, the Ogboni had and still has considerable cultural and social appeal. Fadipe goes on:

> It ... appeals to that love of the Yoruba for organization complete with a hierarchy of officials ... to the fondness for convivial gathering and to potlatching spirit and occasional feasting. Its cultural interest lies partly in the use of ritual sentences and partly in the use of traditional costumes and regalia.[3]

One other important function of the Ogboni is the burial of its members. Usually the society takes complete charge, from the digging of the grave to the dressing of the corpse. Just before burial, non-members, including the relations of the deceased, are forbidden to see the corpse. This has given rise to speculations that bodies are tampered with before they are buried. Ogboni members deny this vehemently. To remove this suspicion, nowadays the society invites relations of the deceased to inspect the body for the last time before the grave is covered. What is certain, however, is that the society gives its members elaborate and expensive burials. This fact accounts in no small measure for the popularity of the society, since in Nigeria burials are highly celebrated affairs. Whole pages of leading newspapers are bought up for elaborate obituary announcements, complete with photographs. Radio and TV announcements are made repeatedly before the burial. Foreigners wonder at this apparent folly and deplore the colossal waste of money. The explanation is quite simple. Nigerians are very religious. Burials form part of the terminal religious rituals for the dead. And in highly emotional matters such as religion it is futile to think in terms of material value. In such rituals man becomes blind, deaf and dumb; consciousness dissolves and that other insubstantial, illogical and elusive part of him takes over. Despairing Nigerians may take comfort in the fact that the great pyramids of Egypt, which today are a substantial part of the treasures of the world, are nothing but tombs. The solid gold coffin of Tutankhamun, the boy Pharaoh, and the priceless paraphernalia entombed with his body are unmatched in splendour in all history. In Nigeria burials are not as wasteful as may at first be imagined. The *Daily Times* and other government-owned newspapers derive a substantial part of their income from obituary notices. (One issue of the *Daily Times*, for example – that of 26 July 1979 – contains fifteen obituary notices. One of them is in remembrance of a woman who died some thirty years ago.) The radio and TV benefit in the same way. Thus expensive burials are, in the final analysis, taxes paid by the rich under emotional and religious pressure. Also, whole populations are fed during burials and in these days of inflation most people are not averse to free meals and drinks.

But to return to more serious considerations, there was at one time a movement to reform the Ogboni and to remove some of its more obnoxious aspects. According to Fadipe:

> The moving spirits, some of them clergymen of the Church of England, were filled with admiration for the beauty of the ritual of the society, and they set to work to purge it of what they considered its superstitious features. The Reformed Ogboni fraternity, as the movement was called, in spite of occasional official expressions of disapproval by the local head of the Anglican clergy, is one of the most influential organizations in Yorubaland today, attracting members largely because of the number of influential persons who are members.[4]

In Eastern Nigeria the most powerful secret society was the Ekpe (or Ekpo) society. The first issue of *Heritage*, a cultural magazine of the former South-Eastern State of Nigeria, has this to say:

> Among the Efiks, the Efuts, Ejaghams, Quas, the Ekois and other riverine communities of the South-Eastern state the Ekpe (Leopard) society has been recognized as one of the most prominent, influential and powerful secret societies of the South-Eastern State. The origin of the Ekpe cult is not quite certain but oral tradition and available information tend to indicate that it originated from the Ekois, then spread among Ododop and other coastal tribes adjoining to the Cameroun and thence to the Efiks and peoples on the right bank of the Cross River.[5]

Although the Ekpe society is not as widespread as the Ogboni, its hold on its area of operation has been very strong indeed. Its functions are social, religious and political, especially the latter. *Heritage* says:

> Before the advent of the British and organized common government in Nigeria the political authority of the cult was supreme; it acted as and was virtually the government of the day. Its rules and regulations were law which could not be flagrantly flouted without serious repercussions. The penalty of death was imposed on anyone who resisted an envoy of the society or on a non-member who witnessed, however unwillingly, any of its secret rites.[6]

The Ekpe society was also used for the recovery of debts, the protection of property and the 'maintenance of the power of the free born over the slave population which far outnumbered the former in some Ekpe communities'.[7] Social functions included burials, games and plays. Membership of the Ekpe society was a lucrative investment, because fees paid by all new members were shared among those in the higher echelons (the Eyamba and Ebunko) of the society.

The Sekiapu society wielded considerable power among the Kalabari and Okrika. It prescribed laws and levied fines on those who infringed them. Its social aspects, singing and dancing, were highly developed.

Among the Igbo there was the Okonko secret society, which acquired prominence in Bende and Arochuku, and, west of the Niger, the Ekumeku secret society. There was also the Mmanwu or Otu Muo cult. According to Edmund Ilogu:

The Otu Muo (the masquerade society) members also perform
some political duties: they guard the village against thieves, collect
fines from people pronounced guilty of offences, and help in seeing
that *aru* (pollutions) are not hidden.[8]

Although among the northern tribes there were cults and secret
societies connected with hunting, fishing, head-hunting and the like,
there were no noteworthy secret societies comparable with the Ogboni
and Ekpe in prestige and popularity. As Meek observes: 'Secret societies
existing for purely political purposes are not ... a characteristic feature
of northern Nigerian society.'[9] One is tempted to attribute this fact to the
strong influence of Islam in those parts.

A remarkable secret society confined to the Kagoma tribe deserves to
be mentioned, if only as a study of the effect of moral considerations on
the formation of secret societies. Now, among the Kagoma a wife was
free to leave her husband at any time. As may be imagined, husbands
consequently found it difficult to retain their wives for any length of time.
Driven to desperation, the men formed the Dodo secret society. The
Dodo was a mythical spirit well-known in the north. If a woman
misbehaved, the husband sent for Magajin Dodo, the representative of
the Dodo society. After holding a mysterious conversation with Dodo, he
would prescribe what the woman should do to make amends; and this
might be anything from asking her husband's forgiveness to subjecting
herself to flogging. Understandably, the women dreaded the Dodo secret
society and did their best to please their men in order to avoid a
visitation.[10] (The Wurkum tribe had a secret society called Zuget, which
was also used to terrorize women.[11])

A recent phenomenon is the development of 'social clubs' all over the
country. These clubs are usually open to anyone who can afford the high
entry fees. They appear to function mainly as insurance companies,
providing their members with protection from the hardship caused by
death and other disasters. Like the Ogboni, social clubs arrange
elaborate burials for their deceased members and pay out money to
support their widows and widowers. The following article in the *Weekly
Star* of 22 July 1979 describe these social clubs very well:

A very noteworthy social development in post-war Nigeria is the
proliferation of social clubs whose membership often cuts across
tongue and tribe.
Usually registered under the Lands Perpetual Succession Act

(Cap 98) and given certificates of recognition by the Social Welfare
Division of the State Ministries of Health, the social clubs charge
exorbitant enrolment fees, sometimes of the order of one thousand
naira. Intending members are also subjected to a formal interview
or introduction.

By providing social security for members and their dependent
relatives, social clubs have proved a formidable rival to insurance
companies. Not only do social clubs pay out large sums of money
within a few weeks or even days to deceased members' relatives,
[but] the club members actually mourn their members. They carry
the corpse down to the village. Where the deceased member has not
built a fitting house in his village, the clubs are known to preserve
the corpse for days in an expensive mortuary and to build a house
before collecting the corpse for burial.[12]

Social clubs may be regarded as open and more practical versions of
secret societies. Their social activities are well-known, but not so their
codes of conduct. The article quoted above goes on:

Should social clubs be banned? I do not for once think that they
should be banned. I think that under certain conditions they can be
made useful instruments for changing our society.

The Social Welfare Division of the Ministry of Health can impose
codes of conduct on social clubs. Erring clubs could have their
certificates of recognition withdrawn.

Investigations reveal that most social clubs have codes of conduct.
Prominent in such codes is the stipulation that members must not
behave in any manner that will 'disgrace' the club.

In most rural societies age groups operate. An age group may be
defined roughly as a generation, the ages of whose members do not differ
by more than five years or so. Among the Igbo age groups are very
important. Most workers in urban areas belong to age groups in their
villages. These age groups are usually active in community
development. However, they may react sharply when a member fails in
his moral duties. If, for instance, a member beat his parents or refused to
care for them when he was in a position to do so, his age groups might
penalize him quite harshly through the imposition of fines.

Generally speaking, Nigerians are much inclined to band together in
social groups. At weekends, in towns and villages alike, innumerable

meetings are held over drinks, peppersoup and food. Members of these gatherings may be drawn together because they belong to the same tribe, clan, family, spiritual church or dance group. With the possible exception of the society of robbers (if such a thing exists), it is true to say that all these societies, clubs and groups generally frown upon any behaviour among their members that is likely to tarnish their good image.

Enough has been said to illustrate the influence of secret societies, clubs and groups in the moral life of Nigerians. While no one can deny that the Ogboni, Ekpe and other secret societies attract people who are very highly placed in Nigerian society, the move of the former Military Government to rid the public service of members of secret societies was probably a futile effort. Secret societies are only as evil as the rest of the society from which their members are drawn. Presumably, the code of conduct of such secret societies should improve as Nigerian society as a whole acquires a higher moral tone. It may be wiser, therefore, to regard secret societies as part of the religio-cultural aspect of the life of the people and to leave them alone as long as they do no discernible harm. Hounding them may serve only to reinforce them and perhaps to disrupt society unnecessarily. The Establishment should heed this Hausa proverb: Leave the hen in its feathers.

Chapter 3

Murder, Theft and Adultery

The tortoise said he planted some yams in his lap and tied the stem to his beard for fear of thieves.   (Igbo proverb)

Improper behaviour is said to constitute a crime when the acts of one man infringe the rights of another and cause him serious inconvenience, injury or death. Examples of such acts are murder, theft and arson. Since crimes of this kind cannot be tolerated by any society, laws are framed to proscribe them, and offenders are punished appropriately. There are other forms of misbehaviour which cannot be said to hurt anybody directly but which, if left unchecked, may lead to chaos in society. One example of such behaviour is incest. Sometimes it is possible to legislate against this type of behaviour. When it is not possible to do so, many societies resort to a simple but surprisingly effective expedient: the concept of abomination or tabu. An abomination, as conceived in Nigeria, is an offence against a deity, who is expected to deal with the offender unless certain rites are performed and fines paid. This topic is dealt with in the next chapter. Let us here examine the first category of criminal behaviour mentioned above, beginning with murder.

Traditionally, tribes in Nigeria meted out capital punishment to murderers, usually by hanging them. If a murderer escaped, his wife or child or some other relation was killed in his stead. There were variations in the method of execution. The Kanuri[1] and Edo[2] decapitated murderers; the Abuan[3] and Bassa[4] forced them to commit suicide. The Abaja (Igbo) killed the murderer in exactly the same manner and place that he had killed his victim;[5] the Kalabari generally clubbed him to death.[6] In some tribes the family of a murderer was required to replace the murdered man. The Kwale (Igbo) required a girl as replacement and twenty bags of cowries as compensation.[7] The Dakkakarri tribe required the murderer to substitute either two girls or a girl and a boy.[8] The Gamawa required fourteen slaves as recompense.[9] In some tribes, like the Gade, the Arago, the Burra and the Ikwerre, bargaining was possible, and the death penalty could be commuted to a heavy fine, usually involving replacement by a slave or free-born. In tribes like the Ikwo (Igbo) the murderer was simply handed over to the family of the deceased, which was free to do whatever it liked with him.[10] Sometimes the fate of the murderer depended on whether he was apprehended immediately or several months later. Among the sub-clan of the Orlu a murderer was hanged if caught but was free if he escaped and came back three years later.[11] (This is analogous to the modern practice, whereby an offender goes free if he is not prosecuted after a certain number of years.) Sometimes a murderer's fate depended on whether he was a stranger or a native, especially in those tribes in which bargaining was possible. If the murderer was a stranger, he was more likely to be killed. Among the Ekiti a murderer who had killed with poison (and this was usually difficult to prove) was only fined, never hanged.[12] The Kadara tribe treated murderers fairly lightly. They isolated them for a month or so, and that was the end of the affair.[13] In this they were far ahead of those modern nations that have substituted life sentences in jail for capital punishment.

Nearly all the tribes distinguished between murder and manslaughter. The punishment for manslaughter was usually the provision of a substitute for the deceased. The offender could also be fined or simply sold into slavery. In hardly any case did he go absolutely free. Among some sub-clans in Igbo the offender was required to bear all the burial expenses;[14] the Edo stipulated compensations for the bereaved.[15]

Punishments for theft were even more varied. We shall examine them in ascending order of severity.

Among the Nupe stealing food was not punishable if the offender consumed what he stole on the spot.[16] The Jarawa tribe pardoned an offender if he pleaded hunger as a reason for stealing.[17] In Ikwerre and parts of Igbo it was quite normal for one person to take a few nuts from another's bunch of palm fruits heaped by the wayside. The quantity of nuts taken was not expected to exceed what could normally be consumed by an individual or, in the case of a woman, what was needed to yield enough oil for a pot of soup. These days when thieves plead hunger in court they are more likely to provoke laughter, but their defence is based on tradition. It must be said, of course, that if the plea of hunger were allowed now, all food sellers, including supermarkets, would immediately go out of business.

For the people of Alanso, Okposi, Afikpo and parts of Owerri it was enough for a thief to return the stolen goods.[18] The Igara, however, would insist on twice the value of the stolen goods,[19] while among the Jarawa the thief had to pay back five times the worth of the stolen goods.[20] In Onitsha and Ikwerre damages were fixed by the owner of the stolen property.[21]

Many tribes and clans did not consider it enough for the thief to return the stolen property; he was also fined and disgraced in one way or another. The people of Oratta forced a thief to climb a palm tree.[22] The reason behind this is not quite clear, but it was probably a way of exhibiting him to all and sundry. The Ibibio commonly rubbed ashes all over the offender and paraded him around the town.[23] The Ekoi tied a thief hand and foot, and if he could not produce the stolen goods, he was fined a cow and some money.[24] The Ekiti chained robbers and forced them to work for the king. The Ijaw hung shells and other worthless articles on a thief and forced him to dance round the town. Thereafter he was fined and flogged.[25]

In the case of persistent offenders, many tribes resorted to maiming. The Bolewa, for example, chopped off one hand[26] and the people of Ilesha one ear,[27] while the Ekoi cut off the fingers.[28] Another very common punishment for hardened thieves was slavery. The people of Arago, Bassa, Awka, Ndoki, Western Ijaw, Ibibio, Igbira, to name but a few, routinely sold off thieves into slavery.[29] Sometimes a thief could ransom himself by substituting a slave.

Among the Ekiti incorrigible thieves were executed,[30] but capital punishment was generally reserved for dangerous thieves and robbers. This was common practice among the Yoruba, the Igbo and many tribes in the north. The Nupe executed a thief if stolen property was valued at more than 10,000 cowries.[31] The Gwari inflicted capital punishment only on foreign thieves.[32] The Kona buried robbers alive,[33] while the Vere practised trial by ordeal, in which a poisonous brew made from saaswood was administered.[34] The Aro (Igbo) executed a prisoner only if he had stolen in the market place; otherwise he was fined or sold into slavery.[35] The Aro were great traders, and for them the market must have symbolized survival. The Ikwerre executed thieves who stole cannons or iron pots.[36] The Ikwerre inhabit the alluvial plain between the Ijaw of the Delta and the Igbo of the uplands and were subject to frequent slave raids. A possible explanation, therefore, could be that the cannon, which was an effective defensive weapon, was a symbol of survival.

We turn now to sexual offences. Most tribes did not draw a clear distinction between adultery and rape when a married woman was involved.[37] Unless the woman was injured in the process, rape was treated as adultery.

The punishment for adultery, as in the case of theft, varied from tribe to tribe. Quite a few tribes did not consider adultery an offence worth bothering about; the Chamba provide an example.[38] Among the Nasarawa tribes adultery carried no public penal consequences.[39] The Obowo (Igbo) considered it quite sufficient for the adulterer to settle the matter with the aggrieved husband over a keg of palmwine.[40] Among the Ekuri (Ekoi) and Ishielu (Igbo) the aggrieved husband was expected to even the score by seducing a woman from the adulterer's family.[41] In Ikwerre some aggrieved elderly men who had neither the time nor the energy to carry out such retaliatory seduction were known to have instructed their younger male relatives to wreak vengeance.

In some Igbo sub-clans (the Abaja, the Otanzu, the Isu) an adulterer was not formally tried, but the aggrieved husband was expected to redeem his honour by fighting the offender.[42]

Fines were by far the most popular punishment for adultery. They varied a great deal, however. Many northern tribes demanded stock, usually cows, sheep and goats, as fines. Among the Burra, the aggrieved husband demanded twelve gowns from the adulterer.[43] The Igbo levied fines payable in cash varying from two shillings and six pence to twelve pounds.[44] In addition, the offender was expected to feast the elders and judges on food and soup made from goat meat. Among the Abuan the offended husband was entitled to one goat, four plantains and four bottles of gin.[45] In the Yakoro clan of the Boki tribe the aggrieved husband had the right to seize the adulterer's yams and to burn down his house.[46] Among the Keaka clan (Ekoi tribe) the fine was heavy – a slave or twenty-five pieces of fine cloth.[47] The Ibibio (Ikot Ekpene) would demand twenty goats and five chickens.[48]

Often the value of the fine depended on the status of the woman seduced. Among the Bakundu an adulterer was ordinarily fined one goat and one pound, but if the woman was a chief's wife, he was fined four goats and the sum of two pounds and ten shillings.[49] Sometimes an adulterer did not get away with a mere fine. The Kanuri, the Gwari, the Kamuku and some other tribes flogged the offender as well. The Koro inflicted 100 lashes, but the offender could buy himself off at the rate of 500 cowries per lash.[50]

A few tribes viewed adultery very seriously. The Igara and the Batta sold adulterers into slavery.[51] The former would try a suspect by ordeal if he denied the accusation. He was made to drink a potion brewed from the poisonous saaswood plant. If he died, he was guilty. If he survived, he then had the right to sell the woman who had accused him or her husband into slavery.

Several tribes classed adultery with murder and punished the offender with death. Among the Yoruba and Edo adultery with a chief's wife attracted capital punishment.[52] In the Koro clan the aggrieved husband had the right to poison the adulterer.[53] The Kugama tribe also conceded the offended husband the right to kill the adulterer if he could.[54] If he succeeded, the relatives of the deceased had to pay damages before they were allowed to bury the body. Among the Mumuye tribe the injured husband might waive his right to kill on payment of seven goats and one dog by the offender.[55]

Women did not always go unpunished for adultery. Sometimes they were driven away from their matrimonial homes or beaten by their husbands.

Rape was more clearly recognized when it involved a young unmarried girl or virgin. The standard punishment was for the offender to pay damages to the parents. Such damages would be at least equal to the bride price that parents would have received from a more patient suitor. Some tribes, such as the Kanuri and the Igara, would thereafter force the offender to marry the girl. In addition, the Igara father would force the rapist to work on his farm much longer than an ordinary son-in-law would normally have been expected to do.[56]

Murder, theft and adultery are still very much with us. There is little chance of their elimination through education, greater piety or improved standards of living. As is well-known, these crimes cut across all strata of society: theft is committed by beggars, low-income workers, members of the middle and upper classes, millionaires, atheists, priests, businessmen, civil servants, painters, technicians, writers, philosophers, kings and emperors. Thus a disposition to steal is not associated with a person's status or estate. Much the same thing can be said of murder and adultery.

However, it may be possible to eliminate certain motives for crime – the motive for ritual murders, for example. This class of murders is committed by people who use parts of the human body for rituals aimed at making them richer, stronger, healthier, longer-lived, invulnerable to bullets and other weapons, or merely to absolve them from abominations that they may have committed. Since belief in the power of rituals to alter the course of human lives stems from ignorance, it should be possible to eradicate ritual murders with the aid of education. Nevertheless, it would be wrong to suppose that this would be a simple or brief process. Rituals are connected with religion, and religion cannot be eliminated, only modified.

Nowadays the Criminal Code takes care of the crimes we have been describing. How closely related are customary law and the Criminal Code? According to T. O. Elias:

> It seems that the Criminal Code supersedes the customary law in point of penalty, though not of substantive law. The customary law of crime is still valid, even when it recognizes offences unknown to the Code. Also, customary rules of procedure and evidence . . . may differ from those of English law; they are however still valid as long as they are not repugnant to natural justice, equity and good conscience.[57]

Chapter 4

Supernatural Crimes

Rather than make amends, the witch gives birth to more witches.
(Yoruba proverb)

In the past certain crimes were interwoven with religion and a belief in the supernatural. For want of a better name, such crimes are here referred to as 'supernatural' crimes. Witchcraft was by far the most important crime in this class. In pre-colonial Nigeria witchcraft was regarded as the most heinous crime anyone could commit. This abhorrence of witchcraft is understandable when the facts (or what passed for facts) are analysed. In the first place, witches and wizards were said to possess mysterious powers that were denied to the rest of the population. This singular and fearsome advantage could not have endeared them to anybody. Second, whereas a murderer or big-time robber usually did not have the chance to strike more than once or twice, a witch could, it was believed, kill several people before being discovered. Third, witchcraft could be used to generate other crimes. A witch could use her powers to convert an otherwise peace-loving man into a raving murderer. Criminals often pleaded that they were bewitched into committing offences. This made witchcraft the 'crime of crimes'.

Man has believed in and has practised witchcraft for nearly as long as he has been a thinking creature. One possible explanation for this is that his mind is so constituted that mystery has a very powerful fascination for him, a fascination which not even the advance of science seems to diminish. Indeed, science itself is a direct result of man's ceaseless efforts to resolve the mysteries around him. Novels about the unknown – about crime detection, espionage, the supernatural – have maintained an undiminished popularity. The film industry would collapse without the element of mystery. *Rosemary's Baby*, *The Exorcist* and the seemingly endless Dracula and vampire series are all-time box-office attractions. Man is an extremely complex creature. He does all he can to eliminate any threats to his life, but, paradoxically, he also gets a thrill out of being frightened and in danger. Perhaps this is his way of keeping his fear mechanism in constant working order, since, as is well-known, a sense of fear is absolutely necessary for survival. If this is so, we will never be able to outgrow our hunger for horror and mystery. One other possible reason for our predilection for mystery is that life itself – the fashioning of living things out of non-living matter – represents the greatest mystery of all, and we are part of life.

This inexplicable wonder clearly suggests that in spite of our scientific victories, we do not know the nature of matter, and that nature herself is the greatest witch. And this is where our concept of witchcraft takes off. For if we do not know the nature of matter, how can we be sure of predicting its behaviour all the time? How do we know that the piece of garden earth in our hand, the blue stars winking at us overhead, the bat flapping swiftly through the night or our neighbour's deep-set eyes do not affect us in some way? Belief in the supernatural can be dismissed as so much bunk without any discernible harm, but in doing so we must not lose the capacity to investigate – for what if we are wrong? Anyway, since our very humanity depends on our sense of wonder, we will always believe in one form of witchcraft or another. For modern man science is as good as witchcraft. (Arthur C. Clarke, the famous science-fiction writer, has said that in an advanced technology science is indistinguishable from magic.) But apart from the products of science, the modern mind has enough of the 'supernatural' to ponder – acupuncture, black holes, unidentified flying objects, mystery cures, the wizardry of brain molecules in the creation of thought, memory and imagination. And by the way: if matter can fashion thought, as appears to be the case, is the reverse not possible?

Witches and wizards were accused of a wide variety of offences. Indeed, in societies in which belief in witchcraft was strong nearly the whole gamut of life's misfortunes was blamed on them. Witches were believed to have the power of metamorphosis; that is, it was thought that they could change at will into non-human creatures like bats, leopards, mosquitoes, crocodiles. While in these guises, they could harm their neighbours. One method of killing that was widely attributed to witches was vampirism or blood-sucking. At night, using their mysterious powers, they were said to pass through closed doors to get to their sleeping victims, whose blood they drank. The victims became progressively weaker and might eventually die unless the aid of an experienced medicine man was sought. Sometimes witches left marks on the bodies of their victims. A wife who was a witch was, people believed, quite capable of sucking her husband's blood at night. In such a case the husband would waste away, while the wife grew fatter and more robust. It was not unusual for couples to separate because of the husband's suspicion that his wife was a vampire. Sometimes diviners confirmed such suspicions. Usually the woman would deny the accusation vehemently, but she might not convince anyone of her innocence, for it was believed that some witches were not aware of their own powers.[1] Thus they could go on causing havoc to their neighbours, and even to their own families, without knowing they were doing so until they were exposed during a witch-hunt.

Witches could cause an abortion and could delay a pregnancy beyond the usual nine months or even indefinitely. They could enter the womb and devour the unborn child, so that a full-blown pregnancy would gradually wither away until it disappeared. A witch with a humourous disposition might cause monstrous births. The child could turn into a tortoise, a chimpanzee or a snail, or it might have two heads, and so on. In 1976 there was a stampede at the Port Harcourt general hospital as the rumour that a woman had been delivered of a snail spread rapidly. A witch was said to have been responsible.

Virtually any illness whose cause was unknown was attributed to witchcraft, especially those diseases that caused the patient to lose weight progressively. To provoke illness, witches were said to enter the bodies of their victims in the form of crabs, lizards, spiders and the like; thus it was quite usual for a sick person to complain of creatures crawling round his body and causing pain. There were (and still are) sorcerers who claimed to be able physically to extract disease so caused from the bodies of their sufferers. The 'extracted' disease usually assumed the form of stones or nails. The sorcerers would show these to the patient, who would often recover thereafter. Witches could also cause death merely by rubbing their bare buttocks on the ground. Even today, among the Ikwerre, it is considered an abomination for a woman, witch or not, to rub her naked buttocks on the ground.

Sudden death, lunacy, crop pests, invasions by soldier ants or bees – witches took the blame for them all. No wonder the punishment meted to witches was unusually severe. In nearly all cases they were condemned to death. The Yoruba executed witches by hanging.[2] The alternative was to subject them to trial by ordeal. They were given a poisonous brew which was nearly always fatal. The Jarawa would ask a suspect to lick the blade of a very sharp knife. If his tongue was grazed, he was guilty, in which case he would be drowned or burned alive.[3] The

Ninzam put convicted wizards into holes and pounded them to death with pestles.[4] The Kalabari drowned, stoned to death or buried alive in a swamp any convicted witches.[5] Sometimes they plucked out the eyes of witches so that they would not find their way back to the human world if they tried to be reincarnated. In Brass witches were speared to death. In many tribes punishment continued even after death.[6] Usually the body was not buried but thrown into the bush, there to be devoured by wild animals.

The Jukun seem to have had an unusual conception of the role of witches. According to Meek:

> It is said by the Jukun that witches are necessary in the world; for without witches the crops would not ripen. The conception appears to be that the mightiest of the witches, having grown weary of eating human beings, devote their energy and powers to the beneficient purpose of increasing the crops and assisting hunters to capture game animals.[7]

Nevertheless, the Jukun executed or sold into slavery proven witches and their relatives. Among the Nupe, too, the evil powers of witches were diverted:

> The Nupe chiefs used to bestow the rank Lelu on the woman who was believed to be the most powerful witch in the village. Her secret knowledge could thus be made to benefit the interests of the community. Turned into an organ of village administration, this woman could be used, in the opinion of the people, to check and control the subversive activities of the other witches.[8]

However, on the whole witches were brutally punished, and such punishment shows how thoroughly dreaded they were. This dread has persisted to the present day. It is not unusual for customary court judges, and even magistrates and High Court judges, to complain that witnesses and people accused of crimes have bewitched or attempted to bewitch them. Late in 1978 a great witch-hunt raged throughout the Cross River State of Nigeria. Mobs moved swiftly to lynch witches allegedly exposed by one Edet Edem Akpan, alias Akpan Ekwong, a self-appointed witch-hunter. By the time the police stepped in several 'witches' and 'wizards' had been killed. Prominent chiefs supported the witch-hunt. The *Nigerian Chronicle* of 29 November 1978 bore the banner headline:

'LET WITCH-HUNTER RIDE ON!' On the front page a traditional ruler, Chief Peter U. Ekpo, the Okuku of Uyo, was quoted as saying in an interview: 'Our people accept the whole exercise.' The newspaper report continued:

> He [the chief] noted that since the exercise began there are very few cases of fatal accidents as against previous years; there are very few instantaneous deaths and very few cases of pregnant women dying during labour.
>
> The Obong of Uyo further indicated that most women in the area formerly barren 'are now expectant mothers'.
>
> He suggested possible police supervision of the exercise so that it could go on in a peaceful atmosphere.

In the end eleven people were charged with murder and held in custody. When the first accused, Edet Edem Akpan, filed a writ of habeas corpus at the Uyo high court, Mr Justice Joseph Ntia, the presiding judge, said in his ruling:

> For many years of colonial rule in this country and the few years of independent government, our government, like the church, has strenuously tried to make every citizen forget about witchcraft practice and to believe that it does not exist by legislating, as in Section 210(a) and (b) of the Criminal Code, yet the belief in its existence has continued to spread, as evidenced in many cases of witch-craft accusations and murders coming before our customary, magistrate's and high courts from time to time. . . .
>
> Considering the other side of this matter, which is the police apprehension that if the applicant (accused) is not detained in prison custody he will continue to carry out his illegal crusade and it might lead to a breakdown of law and order, I have the following comments to make. When the law has reached a stage that one man's preaching against some vicious practice, which practice, according to our [Director of Public Prosecutions], has from time immemorial been greatly abhorred by society and, of course, is today dreaded by society, and yet the society continues now to rebel openly and support this sole preacher against such vice, then I warn those who apply the law to be wary in order not to extol evil practice, but condemn honest and righteous living. For how can the preaching of a sole crusader be so widely accepted by the masses,

yet it is said to be leading to a breakdown of law and order among the very masses?[9]

The learned judge thereafter granted bail to the accused. The Director of Public Prosecutions applied for a transfer of the case from Uyo magistrate's court to Calabar. In granting the transfer, the Chief Judge of the State, Mr Justice Edem Kooffreh, said:

> I therefore order that the case pending in the Uyo magistrate's court on which Justice Ntia had ruled should be transferred from the Uyo Judicial Division and, in particular, from his court to the Judicial Division in Calabar to a judge in the Calabar Judicial Division. I also rule that, in accordance with Section 47(3) of the High Court Law, no matter connected with witchcraft in any shape or form should be filed or tried in the Uyo or Eket Judicial Divisions, because the learned judge has shown most conclusively from his ruling that the people of these areas are rebelling against the law of the land on this issue and he considers that they are right.... Until the law is changed by the legally constituted authority ... the court has to apply it as a duty. For any court to depart from this duty on the ground of expediency or popular opinion is to open society into a wide sea of uncertainty, which may alternatively usher in confusion and chaos.[10]

In the end all the eleven accused people were set free. Part of a report in the *Sunday Tide* of 18 November 1979 (page 3) reads as follows:

> Hundreds of jubilant well-wishers could not hold back their happiness when the Calabar High Court ruled that Edet Edem Akpan and the ten others be allowed their 'escape' back to freedom. The trial judge dismissed the case on the ground that the prosecution had failed to prove its case beyond all reasonable doubts. And with that Edet Edem Akpan walked into the embrace of a happy crowd of admirers in Calabar and at Uyo as well.

This celebrated case gives a clear indication of the powerful grip of witchcraft on the mind of the average Nigerian even now. However, witchcraft hysteria is a world-wide phenomenon. (In 1645, during the Civil War in England, some 150 witches were executed.)[11]

We shall consider next a second group of offences involving the supernatural. These offences had one important feature: often they caused neither death nor injury – sometimes not even inconvenience – but yet they threatened to disrupt society either through the conflicts they caused or through the moral decadence they might initiate. To deal with this class of offences, traditional Nigerian society evolved the concept of abomination or tabu. This meant that any behaviour so labelled constituted an offence against the gods. Offenders were therefore obliged to offer expensive sacrifices, perform complicated rites and pay fines in order to escape the wrath of the gods. For a crime like theft, men punished the offender directly. But in the case of offences classified as abominations, the gods were allowed to take over the regulation of human behaviour completely. Most, but certainly not all, such offences were associated with sexual misdemeanour. Let us examine some of them.

Sexual intercourse with close relations, or incest, was (and still is) an abomination in practically all tribes in Nigeria. A man could not copulate with his mother, sister, half-sister, daughter, niece, first cousin, father's wife and so on. Quite often the sphere of forbidden relationships was very wide. Among the Igbo one could not marry or have sexual relations with anyone within the extended family (*Umunna*), which could include one's entire village and sometimes one's mother's village. That was why before a marriage negotiation was begun exhaustive inquiries had to be made to ensure that there was no traceable blood relationship between the bride and bridegroom. Among the Kona (Gongola State) persons who resembled each other closely were not allowed to marry. It was believed that the resemblance indicated a relationship in a previous life.[12]

These abominations persist today, to the great annoyance of the present permissive generation. Many a young man has introduced his fiancée to his parents only to find them recoiling in horror at the mismatch. This particular abomination has, of course, a sound biological basis. Also it is argued that there are strong psychological reasons why incest is universally abhorred. If a man married his daughter, for instance, his son would also be his grandson, his wife would also be his mother-in-law and his other children would also be his brothers- and sisters-in-law. The resulting confusion would be enough to cause the disintegration of any family.

Many tribes, such as the Edo and the Ikwerre, forbade sexual relations on the bare ground.[13] Offenders were obliged to offer a sacrifice, usually a goat or a chicken, to the Earth goddess in order to placate her. Some tribes, like the Abua, the Igbo and the Ibibio, forbade sexual intercourse in the bush or on a farm.[14] In others, like the Ikwerre, it was no defence to say that the act was carried out on a mat in a hut in the bush. When copulation took place on a farm the offender had two gods to contend with – the earth goddess and the god of the farm. Expensive sacrifices would have to be made. In parts of Ngwa (Igbo) offenders were killed,[15] while in Eddah they were sold into slavery if they were married.[16] The Idoma forbade sexual intercourse in daylight.[17]

The religious beliefs that informed the various abominations are not a matter for debate. For believers, they were valid. However, there is little doubt that these abominations were instituted to regulate human behaviour. If, for instance, sexual intercourse in the bush and on a farm had been sanctioned by the Abua and other forest dwellers, adultery and rape would have occurred more often, and marriages – indeed, the social order – in those societies might have been threatened. It should be observed also that abominations came in handy in respect of those offences which would have been difficult to detect otherwise. If a couple decided to have sexual relations in the bush, there was no way of exposing them unless they were caught accidentally or quarrelled with each other and exposed their relationship. In most cases these two possibilities would have been quite remote. Thus it became clear to the ancients that the only way to prevent this type of misbehaviour was to instil fear of the gods in the mind of the people. It should not be supposed that fear of the gods had no effect on offenders. All available evidence indicates that offenders fell ill or died if they did not perform the appropriate rituals to cleanse the land and themselves after committing abominations. Moreover, any misfortune suffered by the village after an abomination was attributed to the offended gods. And misfortunes were never lacking.

As has already been pointed out, sexual offences did not constitute all the abominations. Sometimes murder was regarded as an abomination, especially the premeditated murder of a kinsman or a pregnant woman. Not only was the murderer executed, but his family also had to cleanse the desecrated land through sacrifices and expensive rituals. Stealing from a shrine or the vicinity of a shrine was regarded as an abomination by most tribes. Usually the family of the offender would expose him and turn him over to the people to avert the wrath of the gods.

Among many tribes suicide was considered an abomination. The usual punishment was to deny the corpse a proper burial. Usually it would be thrown into a 'bad' bush reserved for people and objects rejected by the earth. This was not as futile an action as it may appear, for in Nigerian traditional religion the dividing line between the dead and the living is very thin. The spirits of the dead are aware of what is happening in this life and can be made happy or sad by the acts of the living. (This is the basis of ancestor worship.) Hence burial was of the utmost importance. The following Ikwerre proverb is significant: when a wicked man buries himself, at least one finger will lie exposed.

There were other abominations among the various tribes. The cutting of yam stems was forbidden, as was instigating a wife to leave her husband, touching a woman's leg, stepping on a married woman's mat and using iroko for firewood. A woman was forbidden to step over a man on the ground or to commit adultery while preparing her husband's food, and so on. Punishment for committing these abominations varied. Among the Igbo, as Edmund Ilogu observes,

> any person known to have committed any of these abominations is severely punished, sometimes by being sold into slavery or by being dedicated to a divinity as an Osu, by which one becomes the slave of such a divinity, thereby subjecting himself and his offspring to the most humiliating status in Igbo traditional society. In minor offences against the earth goddess the individual and his extended family pay for the many things with which sacrifice is offered to propitiate Ala.[18]

Chapter 5

Warfare

Until a man has seized the hilt of his sword, he should not inquire into the cause of his father's death.   (Yoruba proverb)

We are concerned here not with the weapons and strategies of war but with the ethics of warfare, as practised by various Nigerian tribes and communities. Our considerations will include the causes of war, methods of declaring of war, the treatment of prisoners and peace negotiations.

As we have seen, various Nigerian tribes made laws and instituted the concept of abomination to regulate the behaviour of individuals. Because of the absence of a central authority, there were no similar laws to govern the behaviour of tribes themselves. As a result, there were inter-tribal wars. Basden, in *Among the Ibos of Nigeria*, goes as far as to say: 'During the dry season fighting was a sort of pastime either between quarters of the same town or between neighbouring towns.'[1] This is obviously an exaggeration.

In the modern world, we note in passing, the same state of affairs exists. Aggrieved nations go to war if they believe that they have a chance of winning. Unfortunately, arbitration in international affairs is very difficult, and in any case nations do not think of it until they have tested their most recently acquired weapons on one another. Poorer African nations with no arms to talk of are more willing to call in arbitrators to settle their quarrels. During the 1966 crises, embattled Nigerian leaders trudged wearily to Aburi in Ghana in search of an elusive peace. African nationals have intervened as arbitrators in quarrels in Sudan, Zaire, Somalia and Chad, often with the backing of the Organization of African Unity. Idi Amin might not have been overthrown if his mercurial temperament had not made any peace settlement with his foe, Nyerere of Tanzania, impossible.

The nations of the world, to their credit, have set up bodies like the United Nations and the International Court of Justice to regulate the conduct of nations. These two bodies are well-placed to judge the world, but they cannot do so because the nations of the world guard their sovereignty with neurotic jealousy. They are yet to realize that ultimately their survival lies in a powerful United Nations invested with reasonable authority, and that it is nobler to be a citizen of the world than a citizen of any particular country. But, of course, as time goes on, economic chaos and the global pollution of rivers, oceans and the atmosphere are bound to bring the nations to their knees and to deflate the foolish pride of patriots of every race, colour and creed.

Since the nations of the world cannot prevent wars, they have tried to do the next best thing, which is to draw up conventions governing the behaviour of combatants. The Geneva Conventions provide for the immunity from capture and destruction of all establishments for the treatment of wounded and sick soldiers; the impartial reception and treatment of all combatants; the protection of civilians who render aid to the wounded; the humane treatment of prisoners; and the recognition of the red cross as a symbol that identifies people and equipment covered by the agreement. The majority of nations have signed these conventions.

Why do human beings make such elaborate arrangements even when they are engaged in life-and-death struggles with one another? Was Kant right after all when he wrote about the Categorical Imperative, that is, a morality which is recognized *a priori* by men everywhere and which demands unconditional observance? Perhaps, but a less lofty explanation may be that in fighting wars nations are interested primarily in establishing their points of view rather than in mutual annihilation, which could easily occur if there were absolutely no holds barred. This general principle of limited war seems to have applied all through the ages. Significantly, a Yoruba proverb says: 'The fact that we are quarrelling does not mean that we want our opponent to die.'

What were the causes of tribal wars in Nigeria? Before an attempt is made to answer that question, it must be pointed out that the tribal wars referred to in this chapter are not to be compared with modern wars, involving sometimes hundreds of thousands of combatants on either side. Most tribal wars featured a few hundred men. An inter-village war would normally involve fewer than a hundred warriors on either side. Casualties could amount to a dozen or fewer, while prisoners of war might number perhaps half a dozen. The big wars were those involving large tribes. The Ijaye war among the Yoruba and the *Jihad* among northern tribes provide examples of large-scale warfare.

A major cause of conflict in Nigeria, and indeed in all Africa, has been

land, on which has depended economic prosperity and, of course,
survival itself. Tribes and communities that have found themselves
uncomfortable in small or unproductive areas have waged wars to
acquire more room. The Onitsha–Obosi war over land has raged for
decades and even now appears not to have been settled finally. The *Daily
Times* of 3 December 1979 carried this banner headline on its back page:
'POLICE BOSS WARNS TUG-OF-WAR TOWNS'. Part of the story
read:

> Four people were hurt last week when both towns [Onitsha and
> Obosi] took up arms to assert authority over a disputed stretch of
> land. The fighting near a pit was another round of the conflicts
> which led to a public inquiry recently.

The Yoruba and the Dahomi fought bitter wars when the latter
launched massive invasions ostensibly to secure more territory. The
town of Ilorin changed hands often as the Fulani and the Yoruba fought
desperately for its possession. Indeed, the Yoruba spent many decades
fighting these wars. According to Ajayi and Smith:

> During almost the whole of the nineteenth century the country of
> the Yoruba was beset by warfare. It was the scene ... of invasions
> from the north by the Fulani who early in the century established a
> base at Ilorin south of the Niger and in Yorubaland itself, and from
> the west by the Dahomi.[2]

The present conflicts in Namibia and South Africa have, in the final
analysis, to do with land and living space. Whenever a colonial power set
out to subjugate a people, its main objective was to acquire more
territory in which to settle, to expand its economic activities and to grow
richer and more powerful. The invasion of the various tribes in Nigeria
by the British did not differ, except in scope, from inter-tribal invasions
within Nigeria. One of the most memorable skirmishes was the so-called
Benin massacre of 1897, in which Benin warriors, who were among the
fiercest in the south, routed a British contingent en route to Benin either
to reconnoitre or to invade. Its motive was not clear, though nearly all
the recorded accounts (written by British authors) of the incident
indicate that the British mission was a peaceful one. The nine white men
and 280 carriers were ambushed, and most of them were killed. The
British party was said to have been unarmed. No doubt Oba Overami,

already under considerable pressure to sign a peace treaty that would place him and his subjects under British rule, must have felt threatened by a squad of nearly 300 men advancing towards his capital. (It is not clear why nine white men should need as many as 280 carriers for the comparatively short journey from the coast to Benin.) Anyway, a quick reprisal followed within a month. Benin was sacked; the Oba was deported to Calabar; and the British took over the administration of Benin. Relentlessly, British expeditionary forces continued the war of subjugation. They sacked Ilorin (partly to establish the Royal Niger Company) in 1897, the Aro and their so-called Long Juju (real name is Chukwu) in 1901, Borno in 1902, Kano in 1903,[3] the Tiv in 1906.[4] By 1914 the conquerors were in a position to amalgamate northern and southern Nigeria. As pointed out earlier, these were really inter-tribal wars, the only difference being that the aggressive tribe was from outside Nigeria. The motives were the same as for internecine wars – the acquisition of territory and economic advantage, lust for power and, of course, the desire for plunder. When Benin was sacked the city's art treasures were carried off as booty. Talbot explains the disappearance of these treasures as follows: 'A great fire which ravaged over nearly the whole of Benin no doubt destroyed most of the treasures, though a magnificent collection of bronze castings and ivory carvings was found.'[5] Michael Crowder estimates that the British took away nearly 2500 pieces of magnificent Bini bronzes.[6]

It was not only alien tribes like the British who invaded other tribes with a view to occupation and plunder. Indigenous tribes did the same in order to acquire land and property and to carry off prisoners for the slave markets at the coast. The great armies of Benin and Oyo waged just such wars of aggression. In the north Usman Dan Fodio's desire for conquest was comparable with that of Napoleon and Alexander the Great, although Shagari and Boyd, in *Uthman Dan Fodio*, deny this desire. They declare: 'The Shehu (Usman Dan Fodio) did not set out to conquer the northern Hausa states; it was never his ambition to become an Emperor.'[7] While this may be true of the leader himself, his followers certainly fought for tribal and political reasons. As Crowder points out: 'Beyond the primary religious motive lay many political and economic factors. Group feelings were of dominant interest.'[8]

Again, when the people now known as Onitsha (Igbo) broke away from their relations in the Edo tribe, they had to fight their way through to the east. According to Bosah, 'They marched through, ravaging or plundering all that stood in their way. They used guns against their adversaries, firearms having been in use in Benin since 1845 when they were introduced by a Portuguese, John Affonso D'Aveiro.'[9] This was a typical migration of a people in search of land and food.

In the Niger Delta region of Nigeria fishing grounds were a frequent cause of bitter wars. The wars between Okrika, Bonny and Kalabari provide examples. As late as 1948 Okrika and Kalabari fought a gruesome war over fishing rights. On 10 November 1949 a Commission of Inquiry was set up to determine, among other things, 'the nature and extent of the rights of fishing possessed respectively by the Okrikans, and Kalabaris or any other person or tribe in the Degema and Ogoni Divisions of the Rivers Province'.[10] Before that a peace treaty had been signed in 1871 by the two parties under the mediation of the British. The treaty was signed on board the ship HMS *Dido*, then docked in Bonny River. Paragraph One of the treaty stated: 'from this date viz the 28th October, 1871 there shall be a complete cessation of hostilities, between our respective subjects and dependents, and a perfect truce shall endure between ourselves and between our successors respectively for evermore.'[11] In 1879 the Kalabari and the people of Bonny, after much fighting, also signed a perpetual treaty of peace under the mediation of the British. Article One of the treaty stated:

> The King and Chiefs of Bonny will not in any way aid or assist the Okrika men against the New Calabar (Kalabari). They bind themselves under a penalty of one hundred puncheons to observe this Article, and the New Calabar also bind themselves in the same penalty not to assist the Okrikas should they go to war with Bonny.[12]

Personal ambition and the pride of tribal chieftains also accounted for many grim inter-tribal wars. The bloody Ijaye war (1859–62), for example, was caused partly by the refusal of Kurunmi, the ruler of Ijaye, to acknowledge the sovereignty of a newly installed Alafin of Oyo who, according to an ancient custom, ought to have been buried with his dear father.

Any direct insult to a tribe or its leader could lead to war, as could the murder or abduction of an important person, say, a king's daughter. The resulting suffering was usually out of all proportion to the cause for which the tribes were fighting. It is so with most wars. A nation or tribe may imagine that its honour hangs on a point of protocol and may go to war, or it may fight to defend a principle, the infringement of which, it is feared, could lead to universal chaos. Of course, principles are important and often worth fighting for, but sometimes they can be grossly and dangerously exaggerated. As the Yoruba say, it is over the question of *jara* (tips for the buyer) that the inexperienced bean-cake seller is willing to die.

There were mercenaries who were hired to make war, like the Hausa mercenaries, known as *dakaru*, who fought not only in Nigeria but also in other parts of West Africa. The Abam, the Ndi-Ekumeku of Western Igbo and groups of Benin and Shuwa warriors sometimes fought as mercenaries in inter-tribal wars. The Aro used Abam mercenaries frequently to initiate skirmishes that yielded prisoners for the slave trade on which the Aro economy depended at that time.[13] Benin mercenaries featured in the Ijaye war.

Usually wars were declared formally. Although it is tempting to attribute this practice to the nobler qualities of man, it would probably be more accurate to ascribe it to the fact that tribes always tried to avoid mutual annihilation. A sudden, unprovoked, undeclared war could be catastrophic. But then what one tribe could do, another could also. So it was in the interests of all that warning of war should be given whenever possible. If one tribe seriously offended another, the offender might anticipate war by taking adequate precautions. In such a case an undeclared war might not be too bloody.

Among the people of Awka, according to Talbot, 'war was declared on another town by sending a message to it by a man whose mother came from the place'.[14] The Kalabari declared war by sending the chief's staff to the enemy. Alternatively, the envoy could carry yams and gunpowder, symbols of peace and war. The choice of the enemy determined the course of events. The Ikwerre declared war by sending two sticks – one fresh, the other dry – to the enemy. If he chose the fresh stick, he wanted life, which meant peace. If he chose the dry stick, he called for war and death. The Ibibio would deposit gunpowder and shot on a plantain leaf on the approach to the enemy town as a declaration of war.[15] The Nupe declared war by sending a messenger called *kuru* to the enemy's camp to deliver an ultimatum outlining conditions and demands, the rejection of which would lead to war.[16] The Jukun did not declare war. Plans for war were discussed in the greatest secrecy by the king and his senior counsellors, and the decisions taken were revealed to no one, lest information should be conveyed to the enemy. Those capable of bearing arms were merely told that they were to get ready 'to go somewhere, to seek something'.[17]

Usually, when war was declared the time and place were specified. The battle was generally fought somewhere along the common boundary of the opposing forces. Some tribes declared a truce on holy days (like Eke, in the case of the Igbo and Ikwerre). Among the Mada tribe (Plateau State), according to Temple's report, a temporary truce could be observed while the warriors drank water.[18] In connection with this matter of protocol in war, the Ikwerre went rather far. When they declared war they specified not only the time and place but also the weapons to be used! These could be sticks, bows and arrows, or knives and guns. It would appear that the cause of the war determined the choice of weapons. A war of sticks could be declared as a result of, say, a verbal insult to the tribe or its leader. Usually, no one would be killed, but there would be a lot of broken heads and limbs. The side that was forced to retreat lost the battle and the argument. In a war with bows and arrows there were a few casualties. A war of knives and guns was an all-out war. The relationship between the warring tribes could also determine the choice of weapons. For instance, among the Tiv:

> People of two minimal segments with an immediate common ancestor act towards each other as brothers and allies. . . . Between segments of a slightly greater depth bows and arrows may be used, but no poison. . . . Between segments of some eight to ten generations in depth the possibility of war (*tiav*) is admitted, as is the use of poisoned arrows and Dane guns.[19]

In general, it may be said that limited wars, preceded by ample warning and conducted with due observance of protocol, were waged between tribes and communities which considered themselves related. Guerrilla wars and all-out wars were reserved for stranger clans, with whom in any case there could be no easy communication because of language barriers.

Except in the case of wars involving closely related tribes, prisoners were not generally well-treated. They were usually killed, sold or retained as slaves. Apparently, an important reason for the killing of prisoners was the great store set by human heads as war trophies. In many tribes they were the supreme sign of prowess. In Ikwerre and among many other tribes a warrior could not take part in certain special war dances and other ceremonies unless he had slain a man in battle, and the final proof of that deed was the skull of his enemy. There was also a specially processed brand of palmwine that was reserved only for those who had slain men. Among the Igbo only proven warriors could wear either the white eagle feather or the red parrot feather in their caps. Another reason why prisoners were often killed was that it was essential to make sacrifice to the gods after a successful war. Also, important people, especially tribal chiefs and princes, were often buried with slaves, and prisoners of war met this need. Female prisoners and children were usually spared the knife and were sold as slaves. Now and then a warrior married a female prisoner or brought up a prisoner child as a member of his own family.

The stereotyped cartoon of the white hunter clad in safari suit and tied to the stake before a boiling pot, around which half-naked natives perform a macabre dance, is not entirely without foundation. In the earlier inter-tribal wars some prisoners of war were occasionally eaten, usually during post-war sacrifices and rituals. Cannibalism is, of course, regarded as the height of savagery – and quite rightly. Most peoples of the world have been cannibals at one stage or another in their history. In China, Britain, Ireland, France, South America and elsewhere cannibalism has not been unknown.[20] This gruesome practice has lapsed in practically all parts of the world except when people are driven to it by starvation. This is more likely to occur in the cold regions of the Earth, where snow can cut human beings off from the rest of the world for weeks or months. In 1846, for instance, a party of eighty-seven settlers, led by a Mr Donner, was making its way to California when it was caught in a blizzard on the Sierra Nevada mountains. Half the team perished while the other half survived by eating the corpses of their dead comrades.[21] More recently, on 13 October 1972, a Uruguayan plane carrying forty-five people, including a rugby team, crashed on the Andes mountain range in South America. For seventy-two days the survivors were trapped in the broken aircraft, which was resting precariously on a mountainside in the ice-bound wilderness. The sixteen survivors ate their friends in order to survive. This incident is vividly documented in *Alive* by novelist Piers Paul Read, to whom the survivors gave exclusive rights to tell the tale. When help came at last there arose the ethical problem of whether or not the survivors, all of whom were devout Catholics, had sinned. Priests had to do a great deal of public relations work to reassure the relatives and neighbours of the survivors by pointing out that it was the teaching of the Catholic Church that anthropophagy *in extremis* was permissible.[22] A firm line can be drawn, of course, between the deliberate killing of human beings for food and the eating of corpses in conditions of starvation. Anyway, the incidents cited serve to show that in all human beings in all ages there has been an instinctive recognition that human flesh can serve as food and that this resource can be exploited whenever human beings are forced to do so by religious fervour, or the pangs of fatal hunger, or both. This unpleasant fact has also been graphically illustrated in a fairly recent futuristic film entitled Soylent Green in which the Malthusian nightmare of an overpopulated world comes true. In it human beings who are fed up with life because of either old age or ennui and who express the desire to die are routinely and humanely killed, and their bodies are converted into highly nutritious cakes to feed the teeming billions. Charlton Heston, the horror-stricken hero of the film, manages to destroy the cake factory in the end. Mankind is unlikely to be driven to adopt such a repugnant system for recycling human bodies, if only because nature already discharges this task in a far less offensive manner.

Enough of anthropophagy. Let us examine another ethical aspect of war, namely, reconciliation. Even the most brutal war has to come to an end sometime. Both parties may grow weary and, by common accord, cease fighting; or one side may sue for peace. Either way, in Nigeria elaborate ceremonies were usually performed to mark the end of hostilities. But before that there was usually some bargaining over the compensation to be paid by whichever side started the war, especially if that side also happened to have killed or captured more men in battle. Prisoners might be released and slaves procured to compensate for those slain. In wars of conquest the winner might exact from the vanquished annual payments in slaves, goods or money. Generally, envoys were respected. For additional safety it was considered preferable to use an envoy whose mother or grandmother was related to the enemy. Married women who were natives of the enemy town were even better as envoys. An envoy from Ika (Bendel State) would chalk his face and tie bells to his left hand,[23] while a Kalabari envoy would tie palm leaves around his neck.[24] A Nupe envoy would wear a white dress and carry a white flag and green branches.[25]

The peace ceremony was conducted along similar lines in many tribes. An animal (a chicken, a goat or a cow) was slaughtered at the boundary as a sacrifice to certain gods. Representatives from the opposing communities shared a meal and drinks together, often from the same containers. Libations were poured, and sometimes both sides swore to keep the peace. Usually, a tree was planted as a memorial. In Ikwerre practically all inter-community boundaries had such trees, which were referred to as *mkpekwnunene*. The name was derived from *mkpekwnu*, which means 'navel', the original point of attachment to one's mother. After the peace ceremony, therefore, the erstwhile combatants were required to behave as if they had a common mother. If, as was often the case, the cause of the war was land, the tree of peace also served as a precise indication of the boundary. Needless to say, a hardy tree was usually chosen. For additional security, holy days (where they existed) were usually preferred for peace ceremonies, for no one could fight on such days.

The Nigerian civil war was fought along the lines of modern warfare, but it might be useful to re-examine it to see how far, if at all, its conduct was affected by tradition. Before the civil war the northern tribes, generally known as the Hausa, had quarrelled with the Igbo, who had invaded their territory economically. The scars of those skirmishes had not healed when the civil war broke out. The civil war therefore had tribal overtones, but it was not simply a fight between the Hausa and the Igbo; other tribes joined in order to secure economic and political advantages. However, the concept of national unity finally eclipsed all other considerations. Moreover, it complicated the attitudes of the combatants. The Federal forces thought of the Biafrans as compatriots, and that consideration tied their hands. They therefore treated their prisoners as brothers, limited carnage as far as possible, allowed food to be flown to the beleaguered Biafrans and permitted international observers to monitor (some said 'referee') the fighting. (It must be said that for the Biafrans these concessions were pure myths. As far as they were concerned, the Nigerians waged a brutal, bloody war. Understandably, there will never be agreement over this.) The Biafrans, on the other hand, regarded Nigerians as aliens. Ojukwu emphasized at every turn that, ethnically, Biafrans were different. This argument was, of course, consistent with his declaration of independence, and Biafrans were urged to annihilate the 'Nigerian hordes'.

Real brutality could not be indulged in by either side because both armies had many men from the same tribes. There were Igbo, Hausa, Yoruba, Efik, Ibibio, Ijaw and Ikwerre soldiers in both armies. Lt.-Col. Philip Effiong, who led the Biafran army in the last days, was of Ibibio stock (the Ibibio were a reluctant Biafran minority tribe that was greatly opposed to secession). Also, civilians of various tribes were trapped on either side. The grimness of the war was a product, in part, of hunger and privation. Although there were acts of brutality and sadism here and there, the civil war did not bear the marks of a purely inter-tribal war.

In summary, one may say that inter-tribal wars in Nigeria have had the same ethical characteristics as may be found all over the world. People have disagreed over food sources and territory, have killed one another, have then become reconciled and have drunk the wine of peace. In retrospect, it is easy to see that tribal wars were futile and solved nothing, which is also true of inter-tribal wars involving alien tribes (colonial wars, that is), though it is often argued that colonialism, in spite of its darker aspects, had the beneficial effect of civilizing former savages. Admittedly, the British adventure in Nigeria, like the Roman occupation of Britain in 55 BC, brought several advantages. It provided, for the first time, a central government to which all the tribes were subject. Left to themselves, the tribes mght have fought bitterly for several centuries before coming together. The stable government enforced by the British gave Nigeria a chance not only to develop but also to learn the art of modern government much sooner than would otherwise have been the case. Yet some important points should be borne in mind. First, civilization, as we know it, is a mere few hundred years old, whereas man has existed on Earth for at least 3 million years. How did the various human races survive to the present day? Who civilized whom? The products of a hundred years of science are dazzling no doubt, but we should not forget the aeons of time gone by and the immeasurable future facing us. Second, it is becoming increasingly clear that modern civilization, far from being the best thing for mankind, may turn out to be a mixed blessing, if not an outright curse. Our lifestyle is not only polluting the Earth but, as Gerhard Krous argues in his book *Homo Sapiens in Decline*, it is also leading to serious biological degeneration in man. Third, man originated in the tropics, most probably in Africa. By harnessing the sun's energy, stored in various forms on Earth, he has been able to leave the tropics to live in otherwise uninhabitable parts of the world. This exercise has taught the inhabitants of those hostile environments how to depend on machines and artifacts whose production in turn depends on the massive exploitation of the Earth's resources at a rate that is far faster than that at which nature can replenish them. It is not unthinkable that our energy and raw material sources may fail finally and that we may all find ourselves huddled together once again in our ancient tropical cradle, basking like the fabled savages in the sun.

In *Black Man's Dilemma* Areoye Oyebola lost sight of these considerations when, under the spell of Western civilization, he laments disconsolately:

We have wasted our own time while others were battling day and night to conquer nature and make their environments better than they found them. While others were running fast in the race for progress, it appears we were loitering along the road. It is sad.[26]

What Oyebola has forgotten is that in this seemingly endless race no one people has been consistently in front. What is more, it is by no means easy to say with certainty who is in front at any given moment.

For some obscure reason, man has never learned from history. If anything, he grows more belligerent and now spends vast resources on arming himself. What is more worrying, it appears that man actually enjoys fighting. It becomes very difficult to dismiss the suggestion that man's pugnacity originates in instincts planted in him not merely to ensure survival but also to check his population. The larger the world's population, the more efficient man's method of killing and the more devastating his wars.

Unfortunately, there is now nothing with which to sublimate this fearsome fighting instinct. All the mountains have been climbed, all the deserts traversed, the North and South Poles conquered. Worse still, science has made life generally easier and less challenging. The only real challenges lie in outer space, to which only a few can venture at a time. Even there, we shall have no other creatures on which to vent our spleen. Alas, Mars, the most promising planet, does not harbour any Martians. Since the journey to the nearest star system will take at least 40,000 years, using the fastest spaceships now available, we are, for all practical purposes, alone in space on our small, fragile, beautiful planet. It is hard not to sympathize with patriots and empire-builders in our shrinking world.

Chapter 6

Slavery

As the rain beats the slave, it beats the slave-driver.

(Ikwerre proverb)

Slavery is an assault on the morality and dignity of man; consequently, the topic compels attention in any study of the ethical evolution of man. It is particularly relevant in ethical studies of Africa, a continent that has suffered more than any other from the effects of slavery. Admittedly, much of the blame for this suffering must rest on the Africans themselves, who were willing to sell members of their own races in exchange for cheap European artifacts.

Somewhere in his evolutionary history man learned to use artificial organs to extend his senses and limbs. Such artificial organs range from houses (a man in a house is not unlike a tortoise) and clothing to tools, machines and domestic animals. Wherever man has found a fellow human being docile enough to be used as a domestic animal he has felt no moral qualms in doing so. It has been up to the hapless slave to liberate himself if and when he has been able to do so, as in the current liberation wars in Africa.

The slave trade was finally abolished towards the end of the nineteenth century. Its abolition affected only the more overt forms of slavery. Its subtler manifestations are still with us. Slavery can be said to exist wherever human freedom is severely curtailed or human labour is exploited. The situation in South Africa provides a ready example. Blacks in South Africa are denied free movement; they are paid low wages that are incommensurate with their labour; and they are not allowed to live with their families in their places of work. Colonial regimes were only a little removed from the harsh South African situation. Natives were generally treated as second-class citizens, and their assets (in the way of natural resources) were exploited in exchange for less than adequate compensation. Happily, the world is gradually eliminating slavery but much remains to be done. In general, it may be said that the tendency of man to enslave his fellow man provides an index by which the moral standard of mankind may be judged at any given time.

Slavery existed in Nigeria before the notorious transatlantic traffic which boosted it. After an inter-tribal war prisoners of war were sold off by warlords and chieftains of the various tribes. It was not only the victorious tribe that took prisoners; the losing side would also usually capture one or two prisoners in spite of the odds. When the demand for slaves overseas arose wars were often waged for the sole purpose of obtaining slaves. Such wars might better be described as slave raids. Surprise was the principal strategy. Those who suffered most were the coastal villagers. As a result, many villages shifted camp to sites not easily accessible by water. In Ikwerre, a clan resident some forty miles due north of Bonny (which was one of the most notorious slave markets on the West African Coast), most villages are situated several miles from the nearest navigable river or creek. Examples are Aluu, Isiokpo, Omagwa and Ibaa. As the coastal towns were devastated, raids penetrated further and further inland. Slaves captured far inland were obliged to undertake the long trek to the coast, where they arrived sick and emaciated. Experienced slave dealers sometimes smeared their slaves with oil to give them a healthier look, which would command a higher price.

Slave raids had serious social and ethical repercussions. In normal circumstances inter-tribal wars were waged to rectify grievances. As far as was possible and practicable, the conventions of war were observed. Slave raids, on the other hand, were unprovoked and were carried out expressly for gain. Man preyed upon man without any moral compunction. At the height of the slave trade the entire West African Coast was the battleground of a virtual Armageddon. This is not to say that there were no inequities before the transatlantic traffic: there were, for sure, but they increased tenfold at the height of the trade. There was an unprecedented disruption of tribal and family life, which became extremely uncertain and nightmarish. The common people did not know whom to trust, for, according to Walter Rodney, a black Guyanese scholar, 'neighbouring chiefs were at times said to have come to an agreement to raid each other's territory'.[1] It may be said that the slave trade paved the way for colonial rule. After the exhaustion, devastation and chaos caused by the slave trade, the people were ripe for the mass enslavement which passed for colonialism.

Criminals were another source of profit. In pre-colonial Nigeria there were no prisons as such, and habitual criminals were sold off as slaves.

Talbot defends this practice with the following argument:

> One of the greatest advantages of slavery was that it afforded an
> easy method of dealing with inveterate criminals, who were thus not
> only prevented from being a burden upon the state but brought in a
> clear profit both from a monetary point of view and from the fact
> that the community was freed of their presence, and they did not
> remain within it to give a bad example or to endanger the lives and
> property of the townspeople any longer. It was also better for the
> criminals themselves to start life afresh in a new country and with a
> clean sheet, where they would be given another chance of living a
> decent life under good conditions.[2]

A good argument, but one with certain ethical drawbacks. Money was
earned indirectly from crime through the sale of these criminals. The
money so earned did not go to the townspeople: it ended in the pockets of
the chieftains.

Kidnapping was another source of slaves. The victims were often
children and women left at home after everyone else had gone to earn a
living in the farm or creek. There was also a voluntary form of
enslavement or pawning. A man could borrow a large sum of money and
pledge to be the lender's slave until the debt was paid in cash, labour or
both. Such slaves were not sold.

The overseas slave traffic had an adverse effect on the administration
of justice. First, people found guilty of crimes like adultery, petty
pilfering and the like, who would normally have been fined, were readily
sold off without the option. Second, even innocent people were hastily
declared guilty and disappeared. Chukwu, the oracle of the Aro, played
a prominent part in this. The oracle had emissaries all over eastern
Nigeria. When there was a suspected case of witchcraft the suspects were
sent to the oracle for a declaration under the guide of the emissaries. A
few days later the Aro agents would return, without the suspects, to
declare, '*Chukwu akola ha*', that is, 'Chukwu has declared them (guilty)'.
By this time the victims would be well on their way to the slave market in
Bonny. The agents would share the profits with the conspirators in the
community. None, not even the rich, was immune to this mercenary
perversion of justice. If a man became wealthy and powerful, to the envy
of his neighbours, the latter could conspire to accuse him of witchcraft.

Accusations of witchcraft, as we have seen in Chapter 4, came easily to
hand. A death or sickness in the family provided an adequate basis for

such an accusation. The people would meet and would decide to consult Chukwu. If the suspect refused to participate, he confirmed his guilt and was liable to be sold or killed; if he accepted, he disappeared on the way to Chukwu. His property was shared, and his wives were sold on the pretext that they were being taken to Chukwu. Even today a popular curse among the Igbo is to wish someone guilty at the oracle of Chukwu. Sometimes a rich man could ransom himself by handing over his slaves to the Aro agents. According to the historian Michael Crowder: 'To avoid certain enslavement the chief would have to pay the oracle keepers most of his fortune, which would consist largely of slaves. He would return a broken man, without followers [that is, slaves] and therefore without status.'[3]

Thus the slave trade had a deleterious effect on the ethics of the people. There was no peace; there was no justice. This meant anarchy, and anarchy produced even more slaves. It was a traumatic, vicious circle that gripped the West Coast of Africa for the three centuries or more of the evil trade.

Let us return to the domestic trade in slaves, which was quite considerable. (For instance, in Sokoto province alone over 55,000 slaves were liberated by the end of 1917.[4]) Domestic slaves were well-treated on the whole, and it was often impossible to tell at a glance who was bond or free in any community.

Among the Yoruba slavery was a vital factor in the economic system. Slaves were engaged mostly in farming. Some served as soldiers, domestic servants, toll collectors and caretakers (but never members) of temples and lodges of the Ogboni secret society.[5] Female slaves sometimes accompanied their mistresses on trading missions; sometimes they went alone. They were so well-treated that they seldom ran away. If a man married his slave girl, she was automatically free. Her children were also free and suffered no political or social disadvantages. When a master allowed his slaves to marry among themselves their children were regarded as slaves. When slaves fell ill they received proper attention, and some masters went as far as to consult the Ifa oracle on their behalf. At death slaves were given a decent burial. Some lucky slaves inherited their master's property and position. They could redeem themselves by paying the price their masters paid to buy them. Part-payments could also buy freedom if the slave could be trusted to pay off whatever was left in the course of time. Fadipe, in *The Sociology of the Yoruba*, attributes the mild treatment of slaves in Yorubaland to the natural kindness of the Yoruba and to the fact that since fertile land, and therefore food, were abundant, the lifestyle of the master did not differ from that of his slave; 'there was no particular purpose in depriving a slave of food simply to create artificial distinction between master and slave.'[6] Yet the slave in Yorubaland, as those elewhere, suffered disabilities. In Yorubaland, according to Talbot:

> A slave had no real position ... before the law; a powerful chief could kill one without any question being raised, but generally he would be sold if his master were seriously angry with him. If he wished to sue anyone in the Bale's court, he had to do it through his owner.[7]

Fadipe agrees substantially with Talbot's observations.

The treatment of slaves in Igbo country was also quite humane. They were employed to work on the farms and to attend the markets. Slaves were not infrequently absorbed into the family; according to V. C. Uchendu, in *The Igbo of Southeast Nigeria*, 'with absorption of slaves into the master's lineage, it became taboo to mention the fact of their origin.' He goes on: 'Although a slave could marry the master's daughter and some slave women were married by their masters, a slave was not allowed to sacrifice to Ala – the earth-goddess.'[8]

Among the Efik there were more slaves than free men and the situation was not unlike that of the Roman empire. The slaves constantly threatened to overthrow their masters. In Calabar they formed a society of 'Bloodmen' (*Nka Iyip*) and defied their masters and the Ekpe society, which usually arranged the burial ceremonies in which slaves were killed.[9]

The Ijaw treated their slaves very well. Although slaves had to work for their masters, the industrious among them could amass wealth, could marry free women, sometimes their masters' daughters, and could even take chieftaincy titles. King Jaja of Opobo provides a shining example. Because of their coastal position, the Ijaw were the first to receive the British, who set up mission schools in Bonny, Degema and other coastal towns. In those days there was much flogging at school, and chiefs, unwilling to let their children be flogged, often sent their slaves to school instead. It took them some time to realize their mistake.

The Ikwerre also treated their slaves well. Often they were employed on the farms. Rich men bought slaves to provide companionship and protection for their children. If a man died before his son was grown up, it was not unusual for his slaves to hold his property in trust for his children. Slaves were also employed in warfare. In this respect slaves from Abam, a warlike Igbo clan, were particularly valuable. If a slave proved disobedient, he ran into serious trouble. He could be resold and used in a burial ceremony. A few slaves served in shrines and were called Osu. This class of slaves were sacred to the various gods and were not allowed to mix with the people. They lived apart, usually far into the bush, close to the shrine of their master-god.

In the north the so-called pagans treated their slaves wth generosity and respect. It was a case of adoption rather than slavery, and many slaves became free on the death of their owners.[10]

The Muslims distinguished between two types of slave – those captured in war, who were usually non-Muslims, and those born of slave mothers. The former could be resold; the latter could not. Generally, the Muslims observed the recommendations of the Koran and treated their slaves well, some of whom rose to occupy the highest positions in the land (for instance, in Bornu all the army captains were said to be slaves or of slave descent).[11]

The Jukun were exceptionally kind to their slaves: 'A favourable slave was treated like the king's own son and fared royally. He could appropriate anything he liked, and if he committed a public offence was generally absolved by his master.'[12]

One common feature of the domestic slave trade was that people hardly ever enslaved members of their own clan. Slaves had to be bought from other clans and had to learn the local dialect. One obvious reason for this was ethnic pride; another was to ensure that the slave did not run away. The first reason is more interesting, for it leads to the tempting supposition that if there had been an all-embracing and effective Yoruba state, say, the enslavement of one Yoruba man by another might not have been possible for patriotic reasons, just as in the Roman empire no Roman could be a slave. If this supposition is correct, then it may be possible to explain the willingness of Africans to sell their own people to members of another race in terms not of unusual moral depravity but of the lack of an all-embracing government. There was no patriotic or national pride to which to appeal. Who was whose brother? The Igbo man was a stranger as much to an Ijaw as to a white man. There was no racial consciousness. To a Yoruba man, selling an Edo slave to an Igbo man meant the same thing as selling that Edo slave to a white man. The white man's country was, for all practical purposes, as distant and as mysterious as Igbo country.

Again, Africa was the victim of a fateful geographical location. If

Africa and, say, the Indian subcontinent had exchanged places on the globe, the slave traffic to the Americas might well have been made up of Indians. Then the present West Indians would have truly earned their name.

It is fair to say that all parties to a slave deal are equally morally culpable. Slavery was possible in those days in its extreme form because the concept of the universal brotherhood of man was unborn. Even today it is not fully accepted. There are people who are still reluctant to attribute full humanity to others. Until this attitude is outgrown slavery will continue to exist, at least in its subtler forms.

Slavery is as old as man. It appears in practically all recorded history. In 5000 BC the Sumerians and Babylonians were said to have kept slaves. The Greek economy and civilization depended on slave labour. Over 90 per cent of the Greek population was composed of slaves. (For instance, in the state of Attica there were 400,000 slaves and 21,000 free citizens. Aegina, another Greek city state, had 470,000 slaves serving 30,000 Greek citizens.) In *The Republic* Plato assumed that there would be abundant slave labour to make his political theories work. There were to be three categories of citizens: the first class was to be formed by philosopher-kings who were to be the rulers and law-makers, the second by soldiers and the third by farmers and artisans. These three classes were to be served by slaves who had no rights and no class.

The Hebrews kept slaves. Abraham had an Egyptian slave – a woman named Haggar, who bore him a son called Ishmael.[13] At its zenith the Roman empire had 21 million slaves and 7 million free citizens. Slave uprisings, known as servile wars, arose. The third and last servile war (73–71 BC) was led by Spartacus who, with a slave army of 120,000 men, captured Mount Vesuvius and held it for some time. Some historians believe that internal friction caused by the preponderant slave population contributed to the final collapse of the Roman Empire.

It is a historical fact that some great empires were built on cheap slave labour. This is not surprising. For a few to acquire immense power and wealth and to enjoy leisure, the majority must be deprived. This necessary privation reaches its limit in slavery. In his book *Human Society in Ethics and Politics* Bertrand Russell says:

> We must therefore admit that slavery and social injustice have, in the past, served a useful purpose in the development of civilization. I shall not consider how far this is still the case as I do not wish to embark upon political controversy.[14]

But for Russell's fear of 'political controversy' in this instance, he might have gone on to say that the USA was, at least initially, built largely on cheap black slave labour; that the British Empire rose at the expense of its overseas subjects; and that South Africa's prosperity today depends on slave labour. In South Africa natives are herded into barracks and forced to work in mines and factories for a whole year without seeing their families. Their extraordinarily low rate of pay by comparison with that of the privileged section of the population defines their servitude.

However, it was not only Western civilization that benefited from forced human labour. It is not a coincidence that the great centres of art and culture in Nigeria were also centres of high slave population. The prosperous citizens of Benin, with its world-famous bronze art, of Calabar, with its highly developed carving and weaving, and of Bida of brass, iron and glass fame, all had large slave populations working for them. As Nadel observes: 'The prosperous craftsmen of Bida town, blacksmiths and weavers, always had slaves to work for them; even in villages one found households with one or two slaves.'[15] Today there are still people in the world, even outside South Africa, who believe in exploiting cheap human labour in the abundant production of luxury goods which the privileged and pampered enjoy. However, such cheap human labour is, in the long run, very expensive and explosive. As has already been pointed out, it is not at all clear that civilization as we now know it will ultimately be good for mankind. We cannot, therefore, justify the promotion of our so-called civilization through slavery.

Chapter 7

Concepts of Goodness

Character is a god: it supports you according to your behaviour.
(Yoruba proverb)

As we have seen, Nigerian tribes made laws and instituted abominations to control unacceptable behaviour. However, it was and always is quite possible to abstain from crimes like murder, theft and arson and still be looked upon as an unsatisfactory member of society. The mere avoidance of bad behaviour is a negative virtue, or at best a neutral one. To be regarded as positively virtuous, one is expected to be helpful and useful to one's neighbours. As I shall try to show presently, Nigerian ethical philosophy emphasizes positive virtue, which cannot be achieved through legislation or the system of abomination.

But what is virtue or goodness? It may be argued that in a book of descriptive ethics, such as this one, a discussion of the definition of goodness is irrelevant. This may well be so. However, it is possible (indeed, likely) that some readers, especially those not acquainted with the problems of ethical definitions, after going through the descriptions in this book, may ask: why does this tribe behave this way and that tribe that way? Answers to such questions are bound to imply definitions of goodness, and so we shall consider briefly the views of a few philosophers on the issue.

Although virtue or goodness is universally desired, it has not proved easy to define it precisely. Ethical philosophers have written lengthy books in their attempts to find a definition of goodness or even to prove that no definition is possible.

Aristotle defined virtue as 'a mean state between two vices, one of excess and one of defect'.[1] Thus, according to Aristotle, it is not virtuous to be either unkind or too kind. Modern philosophers of a more analytical bent might criticize this definition for merely begging the question, for how do we know exactly when a person is unkind or too kind? To know either condition, we must have a precise knowledge of the virtue of kindness itself, and this knowledge is what we set out to seek in the first place.

G. E. Moore, in his *Principia Ethica*, after many brilliant and highly involved arguments, states flatly at last:

> If I am asked 'What is good?' my answer is that good is good, and that is the end of the matter. Or if I am asked 'How is good to be defined?' my answer is that it cannot be defined, and that is all I have to say about it.[2]

Moore is saying that goodness is something which we know only by intuition.

Jeremy Bentham measures the goodness of an act in terms of the pleasure or pain that it brings either to the individual or to the society at large. This is the famous principle of Utilitarianism, amplified later by Mills. Bentham says, with almost mathematical precision:

> Sum up all the values of all the pleasures on the one side, and those of all the pains on the other. The balance, if it be on the side of pleasure, will give the good tendency of the act ... if on the side of pain the bad tendency....[3]

Bentham recognized the limitations of defining goodness in terms of pleasure as when, for instance, pleasure is derived by hurting others, but he insisted that 'even this wretched pleasure, taken by itself, is good'.

Kant's definition of goodness is so abstract and so lofty that one wonders whether he himself had a very clear conception of it. He writes: 'Nothing can possibly be conceived in the world, or even out of it, which can be called good without qualification except a Good Will.'[4] Earlier he had defined 'a Good Will' as something 'good in itself'. Once again we do not receive much help here.

Perhaps we should turn to a modern philosopher. Here is Bertrand Russell: 'I think that the "objectively right" act is that which best serves the interest of the group that is regarded as ethnically dominant. The difficulty is that this group will be differently defined.'[5] With his sharp intellect, Russell was quick to see the defect in his definition. In a country like Nigeria, with over 250 ethnic groups, each of which presumably regards itself as dominant, Russell's definition would not be very useful.

What have Nigerian philosophers to offer? Nigerian literature on the subject is scanty. Idowu, in *Olodumare*, says:

The sense of right and wrong, by the decree of God, has always been part of human nature. Experience comes before theory. That sense was there first, before man began to find the reasons why certain modes of behaviour should be preferred to certain others, and the reasons given are often little more than rationalization.[6]

Thus Idowu believes we have an intuitive knowledge of goodness. He then goes on to list eleven virtues of the Yoruba, among them chastity, hospitality, kindness, truthfulness and the capacity to refrain from theft. *Olodumare* is primarily a book on religion, with which everything is linked, so there is little room for any rigorous secular definitions or arguments.

In *The History of the Yorubas* the Reverend Samuel Johnson has even less to say on ethics than Idowu. Again, this is not surprising, since Johnson's aim was purely historical. Nevertheless, he devotes nearly a page and a half to 'character'. Like Idowu, he lists the virtues of the Yoruba. They are, he says, 'very virtuous, loving and kind. Theft was rare, as also fornication.'[7]

In *African Culture and the African Personality* J. A. Sofola lists the following cardinal virtues as typically African: an emphasis on 'wholesome human relations' among people; a respect for elders; 'community fellow-feeling, as reflected in communal land tenure and ownership'; 'a live-and-let-live' philosophy; altruism (including medical and economic variants of it); and hospitality.[8] Sofola's book is concerned with the totality of African culture, not with Nigerian ethics, but many of his specific examples on behaviour are drawn from Nigeria.

We are left with the impression that goodness cannot be defined with scientific precision and that it varies from one society to another. Thus to question the ethical behaviour of a people and to expect a rational answer is largely futile. Perhaps we should look at Nigerian tribes and examine the virtues that they cherish. One way of doing this is to look at Nigerian proverbs, for, as the Yoruba say, proverbs are like horses for searching for the truth; when the truth is missing we ride towards discovery on proverbs. Every tribe has a stock of hundreds of proverbs, and there are well over 250 tribes. That means that there is a considerable number to choose from, but we shall confine ourselves to a few of those which have a direct bearing on ethics. The choice is unavoidably arbitrary.

On the need for respecting other people's feelings the following proverbs speak out:

The fingers of a man who has only nine are not counted in his presence. (Yoruba)

Disgracing a king is worse than killing him. (Igbo)

When a Fulani is near, you do not discuss the high price of milk. (Hausa)

These proverbs emphasize the need for delicacy in personal relationships.

Very close to the need for respecting other people's feelings is the need for decorum. Certain things, like the offering of cola and wine, simply cannot be hurried. Or again, take the matter of greetings. Foreigners complain that Nigerians spend far too long greeting one another and inquiring after their families, but to Nigerians such greetings mean much. This is crystallized in the following proverb:

The chameleon says he will not alter his dignified manner of walking just because the forest is on fire. (Igbo)

Then there is the universally recognized virtue of gratitude:

Friendship with the ferryman right from the dry season means that when the rains come, you will be the first to cross. (Hausa)

On humility we have:

Bending down to a dwarf does not prevent you from rising to your full height afterwards. (Hausa)

The cook who pounds noisily thinks that the one who pounds quietly does not eat. (Ikwerre)

On reciprocal kindness and co-operation:

The elder who eats all his food will carry his load by himself. (Yoruba)

(In Nigeria it is customary to leave some food on the plate for the children or servants who have to do the washing-up.)

The hand of the child cannot reach the shelf, nor can the hand of the adult pass through the neck of the gourd. (Yoruba)

> If a husband and wife co-operate, one slice of yam makes a big bowl of *foofoo*.   (Ikwerre)

On respect for age and experience we have:

> If a child lifts up his father, the wrapper will cover his eyes.   (Ikwerre)

> A child may have as many clothes as his father but not as many rags.   (Yoruba)

> What an elder sees sitting down, the child cannot see even while standing.   (Igbo)

> A god whose chief priest is a child can easily get out of hand.   (Ikwerre)

In Nigeria respect for elders is considered very important, and a child who does not observe this cardinal article of the code of behaviour is not likely to turn out well. In the first place, his parents will practically disown him; in the second, the children of the elders to whom he shows disrespect will make life extremely difficult for him.

Among the Yoruba young people prostrate themselves before their elders. Formerly a young man in an immaculate *agbada* of white lace who met an elder on a dusty road faced a problem. Nowadays prostration has generally been modified to a deep bow, with one or both hands touching the ground. However, on formal occasions, as when a child is asking forgiveness from an elder or when an oba is being addressed, young people must still prostrate themselves fully.

In Hausa culture it is customary for the young to bow before their elders. Before emirs and other rulers it is customary to kneel on hands and feet and touch the ground with the forehead.

The Igbo kneel on both knees as a sign of respect for an elder, but this custom is dying and is now observed only on rare occasions.

In most Nigerian tribes the young call their elders not by their names but by pseudonyms accepted by particular tribes. The Yoruba youth always addresses his elder with the plural form of the pronoun 'you' (*eyin*) and never with the singular form (*iwo*). Moreover, he is not expected to look at an elder during a conversation. According to Afolabi Ojo:

> To a Yoruba it is rude to look into the face of an elder person when one is engaged in a conversation with him. To do so is to show gross

lack of respect or insolence. This is why raising one's eyes up to an elderly person constitutes a definite category of offence among the Yoruba.[9]

As Ojo points out, foreigners interpret this sign of respect 'as shiftiness or lack of straightforwardness'.[10] This is a typical example of the tragic misunderstanding that can arise as a result of cultural differences.

Generally, foreigners tend to interpret respect for elders as timidity. The result is that sometimes they try to take advantage of it, only to discover that a Nigerian youth can be just as aggressive as anybody else.

Why do Nigerians insist on respect for elders? There are several reasons. First, in the traditional system of education the elders taught the younger ones all there was to be learned. Now, in every teacher–student relationship the student has to respect the teacher. That respect generates the humility the student needs in order to appreciate and absorb what he is being taught. Second, traditional Nigerian society depended (and still depends) for its stability and effectiveness on an orderly hierarchy ranging from the eze, or oba, or emir, or obi to ordinary men, women, children and, in those days, slaves. Young people, like everyone else, had their place in this hierarchy. They came after the ordinary adults, to whom therefore they had to accord proper respect. Third, it is difficult, perhaps impossible, to lead without having had the experience of being led. Young people eventually become elders, and it is important that they should learn to be humble and respectful before they have the chance to rule. Fourth, respect for elders is a direct product of the virtue of gratitude. Every child depends for a long time on his parents and guardians for his education and survival. One way of showing his gratitude is to be obedient and respectful to his parents and guardians, and in the Nigerian extended-family system, parents and guardians can include virtually any elder known to the young person.

Modern psychologists claim that too much respect for elders leads to a lack of initiative in the young. To assess the validity of this charge, it is necessary to study the average Nigerian at work and play and to compare him with his counterparts elsewhere in the world. Until such a study is made, the criticism cannot stand unchallenged. Anyway, the system has distinct advantages. One such advantage is that the properly brought up Nigerian child automatically respects an elder of any tribe or race. If all the young people of the world behaved in this way, we should surely have a much better world.

Let us turn to the virtue of contentment. At first, contentment may appear to be a purely personal matter, but further thought reveals that those who are chronically discontented pose a threat to their neighbours, in that they always tend to push and grab for more and more, making their neighbours nervous (to say the least). Thus a reasonable measure of contentment promotes good neighbourliness and is therefore a positive virtue. In this connection we have the following sayings:

> The fowl eats corn, drinks water, and swallows pebbles, yet she complains she has no teeth; does a goat which has teeth eat iron?   (Yoruba)

> Having been made a king, you begin to prepare a lucky charm; do you want to be made a god?   (Yoruba)

Carefulness and fairness in judgement are esteemed:

> Judgement is not given after hearing one side.   (Igbo)

> Ill-will for the masquerader's guide should not lead one to assault the masquerader.   (Yoruba)

> Find out the dying cries of the man slain in battle before composing a song to mock him.   (Ikwerre)

And on the virtue of truthfulness we have:

> One who sows one hundred yam seedlings and says he has sown two hundred will have to eat his hundred lies when he has finished his hundred yams.   (Yoruba)

> When an elder sees a bushrat it does not afterwards become a lizard.   (Yoruba)

> Truth is better than ten goats.   (Igbo)

> Truth is stronger than an iron horse.   (Hausa)

> 'Perhaps' prevents the European from telling a lie.   (Hausa)

This last proverb was obviously coined in the colonial era. It is a broadside against the proverbial British diplomacy.

Those who condone evil are said to be as guilty as the perpetrators of evil. The following subtle proverbs convey this:

One who claps for the madman to dance is as insane as the madman. (Yoruba)

One should not know one's daughter's husband and her lover too. (Yoruba)

A belief in retribution is not in itself a virtue, but it greatly affects the way in which people behave towards one another. The following proverbs illustrate the belief that whether or not the law catches up with the evil-doer, he is bound to suffer for his crimes:

He who swallows a pestle will have to sleep standing up. (Hausa)

Ashes spread towards the direction of the thrower. (Yoruba)

One who excretes on the road finds flies when he returns. (Hausa)

Moderation is also an esteemed virtue, as is indicated by the following proverbs, in which echoes of the Aristotelian definition of goodness as the happy mean are apparent:

When a handshake goes beyond the elbow, it becomes an attack. (Igbo)

If the fire for roasting a snake is prepared according to its length, the house may catch fire. (Ikwerre)

The funeral ceremony is over, yet the drummer lingers. Does he want to marry the widow? (Yoruba)

Finally, let us consider the following six proverbs:

Both the eagle and the kite should perch; whichever denies the other the right should suffer a broken wing. (Igbo)

My guest should not harm me; when he departs, may he not develop a hunchback? (Igbo)

He who receives things has others who receive things along with him. (Hausa)

The prosperity of a single person does not make a town rich. (Yoruba)

Rapid scoring by both players makes the game of mancalla interesting. (Yoruba)

When other people's goats graze, mine should join them. (Ikwerre)

These proverbs express with varying subtlety the golden rule 'Live and
let live'. In traditional Nigerian society it is a rule which is intoned with
near religious fervour. True, it is infringed as frequently in Nigeria as
anywhere else in the world, but the principle is regarded as the acme of
good neighbourliness.

The extended-family system rested, and still rests, on the
eagle-and-kite principle, to borrow the image of the Igbo proverb. Take
the case of a young boy who lost his parents at a tender age. His uncle
would bring him up practically as his own child. He would give him an
education, which in those days included the arts of looking after himself
and of conducting himself properly in society and basic skills such as
hunting, trapping, fishing and farming. The art of bringing up a family
he would learn by observing his uncle's example. When he came of age
his uncle would help him to build a house and acquire a wife and would
give him funds or the wherewithal for farming, fishing, cattle-rearing or
some other livelihood. When the boy became the man he would look
after his uncle's children, if necessary, to the best of his ability. Of course,
an uncle anywhere else in the world might show his nephew the same
kindness, but the difference is that in Nigeria the uncle would regard his
nephew's education, in these circumstances, as a duty, not just as an act
of kindness. He would come in for the censure of the community if he
behaved otherwise. As a result of this system, the individual was never
without help. No one was absolutely destitute, so the kind of insanity
that is caused by the pressures of urban life and by loneliness were
virtually unknown in rural Nigeria. In a system which had no asylums,
poor houses or old people's homes, the eagle-and-kite system proved
very effective indeed.

The extended-family system also operated at the clan level. As we
have already noted, if two clans thought they were related, they rarely
fought total wars against each other. If war was absolutely unavoidable,
then a limited war would be fought. It was usually brief, and there were
few casualties. In many tribes the killing of a kinsman, the antithesis of
caring for him, was not only a crime but also an abomination. After the
murderer had been executed his family would have to perform sacrifices
and rites to remove the stain of evil and to ward off the anger of the gods.

Several criticisms are levelled against the extended-family system.
First, critics point out that it makes the individual virtually a slave to his
kinsmen. In striving to cater for the needs of so many people, he loses his

own individuality, a thing much valued in the Western world. But then, individual freedom in modern society is largely illusory. In the Western world the individual is still a slave to his clubs, societies and employers and to the tyrannies of fad and fashion. When in old age one's children send one to an old people's home run by unkind or at best indifferent workers, individuality turns into a terminal nightmare.

Then there is the argument that the system can, and often does, impose an almost intolerable financial burden. How can a poor worker be expected to pay the fees of a dozen relations in secondary schools? This criticism does not really hold. A man is expected to do his honest best, not to kill himself in the attempt to provide for his kinsmen's needs. Even in pre-colonial days no one could do everything. There were limits to the help that could be rendered to one's relations. What was and is abhorred is indifference and the spectacle of a man hoarding money and property while his relations roam the streets as beggars. Thus the system can be practised by rich and poor, by everyone according to his means. A poor labourer may not be able to see his nephew through secondary school, but he should be able to give him money to buy stamps to post an application for a job.

Third, there is the criticism that the extended-family system promotes nepotism and tribalism, both of which have seriously threatened the stability of Nigeria. This is probably the most serious criticism of the system and one which Nigerians should not gloss over. It is true that Nigerians lean over backwards to help their kinsmen, often to the detriment of other members of society. However, it is not the system that is strictly to blame for this, but lack of wisdom and of restraint in its application. Let us examine two examples of such faulty application taken from real life.

A chief executive of a government department has a vacancy in his establishment. The post is advertised, and a closing date for applications fixed. After this closing date the chief executive's relation suddenly decides to apply for the post. His application, though late, is backdated and filed with the rest. The chief executive realizes that there are two candidates against whom his relation stands no chance in a fair interview. He deliberately delays the letters of invitation to interviews of the two bright applicants, causing them to report several days after the interviews have been held. He turns down their legitimate protests and in the end gives his relation the job.

In another case a man is assaulted and hurt. He reports the matter to a policeman, who sets out to arrest the offender. On arrival, he finds that the offender is a relation of his. He urges the complainant to withdraw his report and elects to settle the quarrel. The complainant refuses and the police constable turns round and charges him with assault.

In these cases both the chief executive and the police constable probably escaped the pricks of conscience, for had they not done the best they could for their kinsmen? But surely these people were basically dishonest and incompetent in their jobs? The chief executive had every chance to ensure that his relation's application was dispatched in time. Delaying the invitation letters of the two bright applicants is indefensible – in fact, criminal. Again, surely there were other job opportunities which he could have helped his relation to exploit in a fair and legitimate manner? The police constable was downright corrupt. The chances are that he may behave in the same way on behalf of a non-relative if he were offered a bribe.

We are led to conclude that in a modern setting the application of the extended-family system demands more education, more wisdom, more honesty and an awareness of other cherished moral principles like justice and fairness. It is no good breaking one ethical principle in the process of applying another. Indeed, an indiscriminate pursuit of the extended-family system destroys the live-and-let-live principle from which it springs. So there is strictly no dilemma here. We are not about to throw away the baby with the bath water: the water does not, in fact, contain the baby. It is possible to keep alive the useful extended-family system and at the same time to run society fairly and justly. Whenever a man's duties conflict violently with his family obligations, he should declare his interest in the matter and let other people supervise that particular aspect of his job. This is the practice wherever the principles of justice are rigidly upheld.

It may be argued that family pressures can be overwhelming, especially as such pressures are usually applied by ignorant and not-so-bright relations – the able ones get along fairly well without too much help. Now, such pressures can amount almost to blackmail, to accusations of selfishness and of unwillingness to use God-given position and influence to help a struggling brother. These pressures can be defeated by the argument that one stands to lose one's job by being partial and inefficient. It is surely in the interest of the family that bright members should not lose their jobs through nepotism. To make this argument credible, government should set up efficient machinery to deal drastically with proven cases of nepotism and tribalism. The former Military Government took a step in this direction when it set up a Public

Complaints Commission with fairly wide powers. It may be too early to evaluate the effectiveness of this body, but its presence has certainly inspired the common man with a greater confidence in the government.

Enough has been said to provide a general survey of the ideas of goodness cherished by various Nigerian tribes, but we must note also that the hard facts of life and human limitations are recognized. Many proverbs acknowledge that in spite of all efforts, one has to contend with many human weaknesses in a difficult world. This recognition is important in dealing with wrong-doers. The judge who has never committed a wrong act in his life will amost certainly be a bad judge. Human society would be uncomfortable for everyone if we did not from time to time acknowledge our shortcomings and the ironies inherent in the fierce struggle for survival.

It is recognized that pleasure and pain are never far apart – are, in fact, inseparable:

One who has no house has no lizards.   (Igbo)

The camwood that fills the basket may not end well.   (Ikwerre)

The fierceness of the struggle for survival is acknowledged:

Fish do not get fat save on the flesh of other fish.   (Hausa)

If you and your child are on fire, you will first put out yours.   (Yoruba)

Whatever has killed the hen has also taken the eggs.   (Igbo)

It is recognized that the judge himself cannot be always objective, even with the best will in the world. His knowledge is finite and in any case he has his own shortcomings:

Wrongdoing is a hill; you walk on your own and observe that of another.   (Hausa)

The dung-beetle thinks that life consists of rolling matter. (Ikwerre)

He who likes you does not see your faults.   (Hausa)

Even the difficulties of our cherished extended-family system are not overlooked:

A brother is a coat of thorns.   (Hausa)

Again, it is recognized that there can be a limit to love and forgiveness and that even in the most intimate human relationship care should be taken not to exceed that limit:

No man shall take off my gown in the market place then come to my house and offer to put it back on me.   (Hausa)

The crocodile says he feels shy to bite, but that once he has bitten he feels shy to let go.   (Ikwerre)

Having glimpsed what is generally considered to be good behaviour, let us examine how society encourages virtue. All over the world this encouragement is indicated through reward and recognition. Recognition is one of man's strongest desires. All men are vain, and none can resist the bait of recognition. Society knows this idiosyncrasy only too well and exploits it to its own advantage.

The Guinness Book of Records dramatically illustrates human vanity. The book was first published in 1955 'in the hope of settling arguments about record performances', according to the foreword. The publishers soon realized, to their great surprise, that they had struck a gold mine. Today the book sells in millions annually and has been translated into a dozen languages. What is more, the editors have a hard time evading incessant invitations by cranky would-be record-breakers to witness this or that feat. The prize? To earn a place in the *Book of Records*. A look at the book shows that people will do practically anything to earn recognition. Two men slapped each other's face non-stop for thirty hours to earn a place in the book. One man ate twenty-six raw eggs in nine seconds to create a record; another ate fifty bananas in ten minutes. A sleepwalker (he must have been that) carried his bed, weighing 50 kilograms, for over nine miles; another pushed a pram for 261 miles. A latter-day fakir lay on a bed of nails for over twenty-five hours to earn a niche in the book; another kissed a girl for thirty hours. One man stood under a shower for 168 hours; another walked on his hands for 871 miles. A grave-digger dug 23,311 graves to establish a record, but his own grave was dug by his assistant at last.[11] And so it goes on.

The desire for recognition defies any rational explanation. It must lie deep, very deep, in the human psyche.

Before examining the systems of reward and recognition among

Nigerian tribes, let us look first beyond Nigeria's borders. Take first the British, our erstwhile colonial masters. For serving society well in Britain one could be promoted, elevated to a peerage, knighted or presented with one medal or another. Most of the medals are for military service. The George Cross, instituted in 1940 and awarded to civilians for heroism or courage, is a more direct incentive to selfless service and altruism in everyday life. So are the various orders of knighthood. The French have their Légion d'Honneur, established by Napoleon I. It may be awarded for any kind of distinguished service. The Order of Lenin and the Iron Cross are the highest honours in the Soviet Union and West Germany respectively. In the United States, the Medal of Honour is the highest award, followed by the Distinguished Service Cross. All the important American honours appear to be connected with the military.

It may be argued that these awards have little to do with morality. A man may win a highly esteemed decoration and still be a very bad neighbour. It must be borne in mind, however, that society is concerned with its security and survival, and the individual comes after the state. A person who risks his life to save his country is credited with love and devotion for his country, which (it is hoped) means love and devotion for the individuals who make up that country. Now, it would be hard to claim that love and devotion do not rank high in the list of virtues. It is left to individuals and groups to reward directly those who treat them well, and this happens all the time. Presents, dinner parties and kind words are some of the ways by which individuals reward those who are good to them.

The Nobel prizes are global in scope and today represent some of the highest awards any individual can receive. However, only the Peace Prize has anything to do with good behaviour. The rest are for technical achievements in science, engineering, medicine, the arts and so on.

National awards in Nigeria have followed closely the British system of orders. Thus we have the Grand Commander of the Order of the Niger and others. There are, in addition, merit awards for achievements in various fields. None of them has any direct bearing on morals. No doubt, it would be extremely difficult to choose a recipient for a decoration for love, peace or good behaviour, but none the less a national award should be instituted along the lines of the Nobel Peace Prize.

On the traditional front the ancient ways of according recognition to people persist. Nowadays traditional rulers confer chieftaincy titles on their subjects. It is true that sometimes the recipients are unloved members of society who happen to have come by a lot of money, but by

and large a man has to make a substantial contribution to his
community, either materially or by sheer leadership, in order to deserve
a chieftaincy title. Titles like the Ozo in the Igbo tribe, which are
conferred after the performance of prescribed rituals and the payment of
the appropriate fees, may be withheld if a candidate is disreputable. For
instance, a known thief could not these days be admitted into the ranks of
Ozo title-holders unless he mended his ways.

Apart from chieftaincy titles, various tribes had other forms of
recognition. According to Basden, among the Igbo

> men who performed heroic deeds or became famed for their prowess
> in battle were accorded great honour. To such was granted the right
> to wear the wing feathers of an eagle. . . . At his death [a hero] was
> honoured with a funeral befitting a brave old soldier. He had won
> renown in battle and his fame should herald his entry into the realm
> of the spirit world.[12]

As already pointed out, a good burial is a great incentive for upright
behaviour in Nigeria. To a real Nigerian, a good burial is not a matter of
a fine coffin, a decent church service, a decorated grave and an expensive
tombstone. A good burial means the performance of full traditional rites
by the age-group and societies to which the deceased belonged. Some of
these rites cannot be performed if the deceased led a notably evil life.
Further, according to many Nigerian religions, an improper burial
means that the dead man's spirit cannot rest happily or communicate
with other spirits on a basis of equality; above all, reincarnation may be
impossible. These are serious consequences indeed.

Praise names, which are given to deserving members of society, also
provide an incentive for good behaviour. Sometimes during dances the
drums boom out these names, and the men and women chant them, to
the great delight of their bearers. Usman Dan Fodio had many praise
names, among them 'Malamin Malamai' ('Teacher of teachers') and
'Gigani Uban Tambura' ('The drum whose sound exceeds all other
drums').[13]

Perhaps the greatest reward for good behaviour is the privilege of
belonging to one's society. In former days continuous bad behaviour
could lead to ostracism, and in homogeneous rural communities only a
few could survive such punishment.

Chapter 8

Social Discrimination

*Where one person dances and is given money, another does the same
and is given a beating.* (Hausa proverb)

Inequality exists because, first, individuals are not equally gifted and, second, society often discriminates against some of its members on the basis of race, creed, ideology, class or sex. Inequality which arises from differences in natural ability can be partially compensated for by ensuring, through legislation, that every member of society enjoys a certain minimum standard of living conducive to happiness and compatible with human dignity. Inequality arising from discrimination may be curbed through legislation too, but, as is well-known, discrimination dies very hard indeed. It exists in all countries of the world, and it is almost always decried. Even in South Africa, where it is legally sanctioned, there are many people of all races who are fighting fiercely against it.

Because discrimination is now universally recognized as unethical, every country strives towards egalitarianism by ensuring that its members enjoy equal opportunities in such important fields as education, politics and commerce. But, like all ideals, egalitarianism is very elusive. It is a rather ambiguous ideal, in that it goes against the natural tendencies of individuals. Most people are not content with being the equal of their neighbours; they consciously, and often strenuously, strive to be better or richer. Society itself, while preaching egalitarianism, applauds the man or woman who can stand out of the crowd. Again, even in the most democratic and egalitarian nation, the head of state and his aides, the rich, the famous, the politically influential, the high-born, all have a social edge over everyone else, and society condones this elitism.

Among the nations themselves the situation is much the same. For instance, not all nations have the power of veto at the United Nations Assembly. Again, each nation tries to outshine its neighbours, usually by enriching itself at the expense of other nations. Indeed, some world leaders have said openly that in international dealings morality does not exist. They are able to proclaim this principle shamelessly partly because a nation is, by and large, faceless and no one individual can be blamed for the unethical behaviour of his country. On the contrary, heads of state are often acclaimed by their countrymen if, by using Machiavellian tactics, they enrich their own nations at the expense of others.

The clamour for egalitarianism goes on unabated because much of the noise comes from underprivileged individuals and nations, who always outnumber the privileged by far. Those at the very top hardly ever fight for genuine social equality. They may fight for a tolerable, minimum standard of living for everyone, but the last thing they want is for others to achieve their own elevated positions.

Of the two main factors responsible for inequality, the one that concerns us here is discrimination, which has to do with the behaviour of individuals towards one another. We shall now survey the Nigerian scene and examine the various bases for discrimination, with the exception of sexual discrimination which will be discussed in the next chapter.

First, racial or tribal discrimination. Without a doubt, this has been the greatest threat to Nigerian unity. In pre-colonial Nigeria the various tribes considered themselves to be separate and distinct nations and dealt with other tribes from that standpoint. It was quite natural to treat members of other tribes with suspicion and to attribute imaginary characteristics to them. They could be captured and sold off as slaves or killed with scarcely any compunction. War with other tribes was always total. Constituting all the various tribes into the Nigerian nation was a mere political act, which did not immediately affect tribal loyalties and attitudes. (Even now government contracts, scholarships, jobs, loans and the like are sometimes awarded on a tribal basis.) Adjustment to the new realities has been a long and sometimes very painful process. Nigerians, recognizing this threat to their corporate existence, preached against it tirelessly. Glaring instances of tribalism were decried passionately, even by politicians who practised them.

Today, although vestiges of tribalism still exist, they no longer pose a serious threat, partly because of the creation of states. The Igbo still call anyone from the northern tribe 'Alakuba', and the Yoruba 'Ngbati'. The Yoruba call the Igbo 'Kobokobo' and the Hausa-speaking tribes 'Gambari'. The Hausa call the Igbo 'Nyamiri' and the Yoruba 'Bayerebi'. Originally these nicknames were loaded with contempt, ridicule and aggression. Today they are more a source of amusement and jokes than anything else. Nevertheless, Nigerians have not assumed that tribalism is dead and so have not relaxed their vigilance. The new Nigerian Constitution, for instance, makes it practically impossible for a candidate to win the presidential election through tribal influence alone. Paragraph 126(2) of the Constitution stipulates that:

> A candidate for an election to the office of President shall be deemed to have been duly elected to such office where there being more than two candidates for the election:-
> (a) he has the highest number of votes cast at the election; and
> (b) he has not less than one-quarter of the votes cast at the election in each of at least two-thirds of all the states in the Federation.

Now, by popular reckoning there are at least 150 different tribes in two-thirds of the Federation. Thus, a winning candidate will have to be popular with the majority of tribes. (Incidentally, during the 1979 presidential election, a crisis arose over the correct interpretation of two-thirds of nineteen states. It was finally resolved by a rigid mathematical solution, that is, two-thirds was deemed to be $12\frac{2}{3}$. Thus, in the thirteenth state the presidential candidate needed to score only a quarter of two-thirds of the votes cast. The successful candidate, Alhaji Shehu Shagari, made it by the skin of his teeth.) Also a president must choose at least one minister from each of the nineteen states of the Federation. Similar constraints are applied to the state governors.

The Nigerian situation is not unique. All multi-tribal nations face the same problem. Tribal problems exist in Kenya, Uganda, Sierra Leone and even in Britain, where Irish, English, Scottish, Welsh and, recently, black sentiments are still to be reckoned with in national affairs. Tribalism becomes more acute when not merely different tribes but different races are citizens of the same country. The Americas, South Africa, Kenya, Zimbabwe and Britain, to mention a few, still have to solve the problem of persuading their various racial groups to behave decently towards one another.

Religious discrimination was practically unknown among the tribes until foreign religions were introduced. Most tribes respected one another's gods and made no attempt whatsoever at conversion. On the contrary, the mysteries surrounding any particular religion were jealously guarded against intruders. It is true that practitioners of local religions sometimes abused their offices for gain, as in the case of the agents of Chukwu (the so-called 'Long Juju') of Arochukwu, who sold those who sought divination into slavery, but this was not the same thing as discrimination and intolerance in daily life. Both Moslems and Christians made it their business to convert people of other religions. Despite the talk about saving souls, conversion implies a certain amount of intolerance. It means that the converter cannot put up with a neighbour who holds to another creed and so does his best to bring him to accept his faith. In the southern part of Nigeria the early Christians destroyed the shrines of indigenous gods by sheer force and sometimes blackmailed the worshippers of other gods into accepting baptism. The situation was worsened by the fact that the early Christians confused religion with culture, and in their crusade against what they called 'heathenism' they destroyed works of art and banned cultural dances and time-honoured rituals which provided peep-holes into the remote past.

The prestigious Ozo institution of the Igbo was one of the few traditional institutions that resisted the Christian onslaught. For once the native culture fought back gallantly, and the tradition was preserved, but the Catholic Church is still trying to devise a Christian version of the institution.[1] In the north the Moslems fought *Jihads*, or holy wars, in their bid to convert others to their faith. The *Jihad* had the same unfortunate effects as the Christian Crusade.

Happily, these days the zeal of conversion has cooled somewhat. There are still Jehovah's Witnesses who go from door to door compelling otherwise indifferent citizens to listen to their sermons; there are revival groups who pitch their tents in public parks and preach all night over powerful loudspeakers; and there are Moslems who promise would-be converts free trips to Mecca. Among ordinary citizens, however, there is little or no discrimination on religious grounds in the social, political and economic spheres of daily living.

Closely resembling religious discrimination was the discrimination practised by members of secret societies. In pre-colonial Nigeria members of secret societies often regarded themselves as superior to the rest of the populace. Sometimes the effect of this superiority complex went beyond mere incivility to neighbours, as when secret societies denied other people the use of public highways when masquerading, causing non-members to flee for their lives at the mere sight of their masquerades. Anyone who stood his ground paid dearly for his impudence. The Ekumeku Society, west of the Niger, overplayed its hand when its members began to harass the early Christians. The British colonial administration had to organize an offensive against the members and virtually eliminated them. The Sekiapu Society of Tombia, a clan in Kalabari, provides an illuminating example of the type of discrimination we have been discussing. The society had ten rules, three of which were as follows:

Anyone who asked the club or members that [who?] are you, liable to pay four shillings.

Any person who are not one of the Sekki-Apu's club and wear feather in the public, liable to pay five shillings.

Any person who sing Sekki-Apu's song in the town, liable to pay two shillings.[2]

Thus members of this society sought to control what non-members said, what dress they wore and what songs they sang.

Members of secret societies continue to show kindness to one another, as one would expect, but it is difficult to assess how far such kindness puts non-members at a disadvantage, which is an indication that discrimination based on secret societies is minimal in modern Nigeria.

Apart from the special case of members of secret societies, who regarded themselves as special citizens, discrimination based on social status has also been minimal because class-consciousness has never been strong in Nigeria. Even now that an educated middle class has emerged, the extended family system ties the rich man securely to his poor relations, some of whom may have contributed towards his education. He is unable to look down on the poor because he is very closely associated with them. Moreover, the chances are that at one time he himself wallowed in that same grinding poverty.

Pre-colonial Nigeria had no identifiable political ideology. Even today Nigerians are not ideologically conscious, and one can say that there is no discrimination based on ideological grounds. There are no ideological differences between the various political parties. Voting is influenced largely by personalities and tribes.

However, there is considerable discrimination on the basis of political parties. Just before, during and soon after political elections less enlightened political opponents sometimes cease to be on speaking terms. Fights and court cases are still frequent. In 1965, on the eve of the

Civil War, people committed heinous offences, which they would normally consider abominable, like pouring petrol on political opponents and setting them alight. After the last civilian presidential elections, some states controlled by parties opposed to the President's refused to exhibit the President's picture in their states. Again, greater job opportunities were offered to supporters of the parties in power, not only in political but even in Civil Service appointments. Records of votes cast in the election were carefully preserved. Public servants who came from areas in which the ruling party scored very few votes were blamed and victimized. Before the Civil War some political parties were known to have withdrawn social services like pipe-borne water from communities in which their candidates failed.

These unethical practices arise from a misconception of what leadership in the modern world is all about. Winning an election sometimes becomes an end in itself. Defeat at the polls is taken to be a personal affront, as if the populace had no right to choose its leaders. These malpractices may be the growing pains and tears of a nation learning modern democracy, but they certainly have an effect on Nigerian ethics. It is no excuse to say that elsewhere in the world murders and assassinations are committed for political motives. It would be fascinating to examine closely the reasons for such antisocial behaviour in the game of politics, but such a study lies outside the scope of this book.

Chapter 9

Sexual Discrimination

You cannot please a woman even if you pierce a stone and hang it round her neck.
(Igbo proverb)

Like tribal discrimination, discussed in the previous chapter, sexual discrimination has a biological basis, but it is more serious because it involves the entire human race. One may join a secret society, or move up the social ladder, or become assimilated into another culture and so escape the corresponding forms of discrimination, but in spite of the antics of a few adventurous surgeons attempting sex-change operations, one cannot escape from one's sex and so cannot escape sexual discrimination if one lives where it exists.

Discrimination affects both sexes, but women have suffered far more from it. That fact cannot be denied. Most legal codes pay special attention to women. This implies that it is generally realized that they need to be protected not only from physical harm but also from discriminatory practices of which they are the victims.

Men and women need each other emotionally and, of course, for survival. It is strange, therefore, that in spite of this unavoidable interdependence, discrimination exists between them. No psychologist or anthropologist has come up with a completely satisfactory explanation for this phenomenon.

The problems of women arise from two factors. The first is their relative muscular weakness. According to studies conducted by the War Department of the United States, women have only 55 per cent of the muscle strength and 67 per cent of the endurance of men.[1] This means that the average man can overpower the average woman in an unarmed duel. When, therefore, an urgent struggle for survival arises – that is, a struggle that involves escape from immediate personal danger – a woman is usually at a disadvantage unless, as is often the case, she is given special consideration. Emergencies aside, the milder daily struggle for survival goes on all the time, and men who are not unduly concerned with morals tend to ride rough-shod over unprotected women. Incidentally, it must be borne in mind that muscular superiority is not the same thing as constitutional superiority, for it has been demonstrated scientifically that in many ways women are tougher than men. For one thing they live longer. Thus in the survival game women are not at an overall disadvantage. Again, it is possible that as we get deeper and deeper into the push-button and robot age, even man's muscular advantage may be completely neutralized.

The second problem facing women has to do with their most vital function, childbirth. For the nine months in which a woman is pregnant, and for a few weeks afterwards, she is relatively helpless and needs the active assistance of men. Now, anyone who has predictable periods of weakness is unlikely to be in a position to dictate terms unless he or she has other powers to counterbalance such a disadvantage. Women, as we shall see later, do have such compensatory powers, but by all indications they are not enough to prevent men's domination.

Sexual discrimination at the personal level is tolerable, though annoying. All a woman has to do is to avoid men who ill-treat her as much as possible. Institutionalized sexual discrimination is a far more serious matter, for it makes women second-class citizens, and this is what feminists are fighting against. Thanks to their militancy, the plight of women has now been more widely recognized. All over the world successive legislation has considerably improved the lot of women, but, ironically, as women press harder and harder for equal rights, they appear to run into difficulties in certain areas. Laws are not only ethical but also logical; consequently, when women score points for themselves quite often they find that they have also scored a point either against themselves or for men. For instance, the exclusion of women from certain categories of military duty must be deemed discriminatory and inconsistent with the principle of strict equality between the sexes. And yet common sense indicates that this practice is necessary to protect women from unnecessary hardship. When President Jimmy Carter of the United States decided to register and draft both sexes into the army, feminists opposed registration and the draft for all but claimed that if men were required to register, women should be too. Anti-feminists blamed the idea of drafting women on the women's liberation movement and charged that President Carter had 'stabbed American womanhood in the back in a cowardly surrender to women's lib'.[2]

We may note here that in ancient Nigeria women of certain tribes went to war alongside their menfolk. In Aboh, according to Nzimiro:

Women also played important roles in warfare. They had their own war fleet and their commanders of these canoes carried special fans (azuzu) which, according to their belief, warded off the bullets of the enemy. They did not engage in fighting, but they accompanied the fleet singing special war songs.[3]

Again, the demand for strict equality necessarily means repudiating some of the concessions already made to women on the grounds of their assumed inequality. The payment of alimony, the opening of doors for women and the giving up of seats to women are some examples of such legal and conventional concessions. No doubt, equitable solutions will be found to this dilemma, but things are not made any easier by women anti-feminists who consider that it is not in their interests to press for strict equality with men.

Although Nigeria is a man's country, there have been several outstanding women. Queen Amina of Zaria is a notable example. She ruled Zaria for thirty-four years early in the fifteenth century, and under her that kingdom became the most powerful in central Sudan.[4] And today there are highly industrious and influential market women who can hold their own against their menfolk; there are women Ministers of State, top government officials and business executives. But there are also women in purdah in some parts of the Muslim north and, among some Yoruba, women who must kneel whenever they bring food to their husbands.

Yet the feminist movement has not been totally absent from Nigeria. As far back as 1929 there was a spectacular demonstration of women's resentment against oppression (or what they regarded as such). This incident, popularly referred to as the Aba Women's War, was initiated by Igbo women who interpreted a headcount of women as a first step towards forcing them to pay tax. Although they were mistaken, one could not blame them, for a previous headcount of men had, in fact, resulted in the payment of tax by men, even though no one had been told that the count was for that purpose. The demonstration which began in Aba and Owerri spread rapidly over much of the then Eastern Provinces, including Calabar and Opobo. The colonial administration was shocked at the efficiency with which otherwise docile women mobilized and organized themselves without any help from their men.

Although a few women carried matchets, most were unarmed. They relied entirely on their bodies for protection. Many of them were said to have been half-naked and to have walked and danced in an obscene manner. Some men were said to have taken fright and to have fled at the sight of the marching women. The women were right in their forecast that their naked bodies and brazen behaviour would scare their menfolk. It was an unnerving demonstration of their uncanny insight into men's psychology. Pressing their luck, the women sacked court buildings and physically assaulted warrant chiefs, whom they accused of oppression and corruption – and quite rightly. Commenting on the uprising, an old Ikwerre woman gave a startling and rather mythical account of it. She said that she herself did not take part because she was too young and scared to do so. As the endless columns of the Amazons approached, men fled into their houses or into the nearest bush. She said the Amazons were terrible to behold. They had mystical powers which made them bullet-proof. When they wanted to rest, they merely pulled at their ears, which extended, rubber-like, to the ground and formed mats, on which they sat. There was an unmistakable glow of pride in her eyes as she sang one of the Igbo songs with which she said the Amazons had marched through her village:

O gini bu iwe?	What annoys us?
Takisi bu iwe.	Tax annoys us.
O gini bu iwe?	What annoys us?
Takisi bu iwe.	Tax annoys us.
Onye si nwayi tu ego?	Who says women should pay tax?
Onye nyere nwayi ego?	Who gave women money?

The colonial administration could not tolerate this state of affairs for long. The order to open fire on the women was given on 16 December 1929 at Opobo, and in all fifty-three women were killed in Calabar Province alone.[5] Gailey observes that although the women failed in their immediate objective,

> they did force the British government to investigate carefully indirect rule in Eastern Nigeria. Then for the first time, despite the many previous ordinances and proclamations, officials at all levels tried to understand the complex social and political systems of the Ibo and Ibibio.[6]

The Women's War was an act of defiance directed against the colonial administration and its local agents. Let us now examine some acts of discrimination suffered by women within the traditional framework. Marriage is a good starting point.

In ancient Nigeria a wife was regarded as the husband's property. The man paid a certain amount as bride-price, and the woman became his. (Incidentally, this is the reverse of the European custom by which a woman 'buys' the man by bringing a dowry.) She bore his name, and her children belonged to him. If for any reason she divorced him, she or her people would have to pay back the bride-price *in full*, in spite of the fact that she might have spent the best part of her life in the man's service and might have borne him children. The inequity is obvious. Among the Gwari tribe, marriage was effected by capture. A young man waylaid the girl he fancied and, with the help of his friends, captured her and took her to his home. After some three days he could carry gifts to her father and tell him what had happened. If the father accepted the gifts, the marriage was on. Otherwise the girl was returned, and the young bachelor prepared for yet another ambush.[7]

A woman was expected to arrive at her husband's house a virgin, and during marriage fidelity was required of her. No such demands were made on the man. In many parts of Nigeria an unwed mother suffered much anguish and was ridiculed; not so an unwed father. At the worst he would be asked to marry the woman, but no stigma was attached to his behaviour.

In ancient Nigeria, a widow suffered much during the mourning period, which usually lasted for about a year. She was not allowed to do her hair, wash her clothes or even bathe regularly. In extreme cases she was buried with her husband. For men who lost their wives, on the other hand, there was hardly any recognized traditional period of mourning. A widower could, in fact, marry another wife within a matter of weeks after his wife's death.

In general, women were not entrusted with leadership. It was believed that they could not keep secrets or maintain their resolve. So the men always had greater social and political powers. There were a few exceptions here and there. According to Talbot,

> owing to the Ake juju among the Bini, the Ekpa of the Central Cross-River and the Nimm society among the Ekoi, the women of these regions are in many ways more powerful than the men, who are much too afraid to ill-treat them.[8]

Also among the Jukun there is a high-ranking woman known as Angwu Tsi:

> [She] is regarded as a queen, the female counterpart of the king. . . .
> She is the head of the female population and her palace is an asylum
> for all who have incurred the king's displeasure. She exercises
> certain priestly functions among which is the duty of formally
> planting the royal seed each year.[9]

And among the Nupe there used to be women officers of state known as
Sagi, who occupied extremely influential positions in the king's court:

> They took part in the king's council, they could join the war with
> other troops of slaves and serfs, they held fiefs and owned land.[10]

The falsehood of the notion that women are incapable of ruling has, of
course, been very amply demonstrated in modern times. However, in
Nigeria today sexual discrimination is still very much alive. There is a
tendency to exclude women from key posts in government and business.
Men argue that there are not enough qualified women to go round. If this
is so, then it is partly a result of the reluctance, particularly in the past, to
educate women. On the other hand, it is true to say that quite a high
proportion of Nigerian women prefer running their homes to pursuing
careers outside; but then Nigerian feminists argue that even this attitude
is a result of poor education. They are not entirely right, for they ignore
certain intractable problems. The great responsibilities of women
– childbirth and child-rearing – are so demanding that so far no
substitute for mothers has been found. There have been inventions
designed to release men from physical drudgery and to leave them freer
for the pursuit of politics, trade, the arts and even large-scale warfare
but, as Margaret Mead points out: 'Where technology and new sources
of power freed men, they did not free women.' She goes on:

> Equal education, political suffrage, freedom of occupation, the right
> to ownership of property, freedom of divorce, the freedom to live an
> independent life, however necessary, are not satisfactory solutions
> to the problem of how women are to make contributions as
> individual human beings as well as in their roles as wives and
> mothers and maintainers of the minutiae of individual lives.[11]

Child-rearing is a complicated and full-time job while it lasts. The
woman who wants to raise a family and at the same time makes a career
for herself may be equated to the man who wants to be proficient in two

professions simultaneously. Day-care centres for the babies of working
mothers and a more active involvement of men in the chores of
child-rearing could improve the lot of women considerably; but it is hard
to deny that the mother has a special role which no one else can
satisfactorily play. There is breastfeeding, for instance. And there is also
that subtle emotional bond between mother and child which cannot be
interfered with without causing serious psychological damage to the
child. Many men are convinced of this, and this conviction may be one
possible explanation for their persistent attempts to discourage women
from taking up careers outside the home. Feminists, of course, disagree
entirely. As far as they are concerned, men want to restrict women to the
home purely in order to dominate them.

Only a few years ago a single woman lost her government job if she
became pregnant, but the bachelor who fathered the child was left
unscathed. Section 03305 of the Old General Orders of the Nigerian
Federation states: 'Any unmarried woman servant may be required to
resign her appointment if she becomes pregnant. A woman servant who
becomes pregnant may therefore be required to produce evidence of her
marriage.' The law has now caught up with this inequity. However, girls
in secondary schools are still faced with this problem. They are forced to
terminate their education if they become pregnant. As a result, there are
proportionately more drop-outs among girls tham among boys. There is
no reason – other than discriminatory practice – why a girl should not
continue with her education after her baby is delivered. The hope that
this injustice to girls will discourage immorality is vain because boys,
who are usually the aggressive parties, are not punished in the same way
and so will continue to seduce girls.

In a pamphlet entitled *Laws and Customs Affecting Women's Status in
Nigeria*, Dr J. O. Akande lists the following disadvantages, among many
others, suffered by women under civil law:

1. A married woman cannot control her own property especially if
   the property is acquired after marriage. Therefore she cannot
   legally make contracts in respect of her property if this will
   jeopardize the husband's right in such property.

2. She cannot enter into loan or hire-purchase agreements without
   the husband's consent.

3. She cannot obtain a passport without the husband's consent.

There is no law requiring such consent but administrative practice.

4. Her domicile follows that of the husband, therefore, during the subsistence of the marriage, she is merely an appendage of the husband and not an individual, e.g. a woman living in Nigeria cannot start divorce proceedings against her husband if he is living outside Nigeria.[12]

Although men argue, sometimes with justification, that women are unfit for certain jobs, they do not hesitate to grab even those jobs which ideally should be done by women. The field of gynaecology, for instance, is flooded with men. Again, men say that a woman's place is in the kitchen, but the world's great chefs are men.

Religous discrimination against women is minimal. There are many priestesses in traditional Nigerian religion, although some of the famous gods, such as Amadioha, Chukwu and Igwekala, are always served by men priests. Admittedly, not much can be done in this area, for the gods themselves are supposed to elect their priests. The imported religions are much more discriminating than the native ones. The Pope is rigidly opposed to accepting women for the priesthood in spite of the rebellion of some American Roman Catholic sects on the issue. The Anglican Church is still dragging its feet on the matter, although it seems more flexible.

Do Nigerian men suffer any sexual discrimination? Perhaps, but certainly not as much as the women. It is true that men go to war, but then wars break out only once in a while. In any case, the risks of childbirth are probably comparable with the risks of war, and childbirth is a continual process.

Young Fulani men have to undergo the ordeal of whipping before marriage. This is supposed to test whether a marriage candidate is man enough to take on the burdens of marriage. But then it is not the women who require or administer the flogging. If men undertake to flog themselves, that can hardly be classed as discrimination.

If men are so sure of their powers, why do they go to such lengths to discriminate against women, who are their life-long and inseparable companions? There are two possible reasons: either men hate women or they fear them. The possibility of hatred must be ruled out in view of the strong emotional bond between the sexes. It must be, then, that men fear women. Why? Fear is generated only by the realization that the feared object has more power than one can cope with. It is suggested here that men discriminate against women because they believe women have a power which they cannot match or control. This power is obviously sexual power. Every woman has it, and every normal man is susceptible to it. The power is awesome because women cannot be deprived of it. Moreover, it operates all the time. Man cannot – indeed, is not inclined to – design any armour against it. Yet it irks him to think that a companion who is otherwise so weak can dominate him completely with this naturally endowed power.

Because man recognizes instinctively that feminine sexual powers are overwhelming, he is reluctant to concede any further powers and privileges to woman. More than that, he actively seeks to reduce her powers by discrimination and other forms of unethical treatment. A successful middle-aged farmer, commenting on this matter, said he was convinced that his three wives controlled him more than he controlled them. They dictated what he ate, and what greater power could anyone have over another? As for sex, when they withheld it he virtually had to crawl on his knees to them, for flogging would not work. He was convinced that men's domination over women was mostly 'by mouth', that is, more apparent than real. To make this point he told a story. This anecdote is almost certainly apocryphal or at best grossly exaggerated, a reproduction of the imagination rather than of fact; but that makes it more remarkable, for it provides a vivid Freudian revelation of men's subconscious fears of female sexuality. The story is reproduced ungarnished.

In eastern Nigeria there are men who hawk chickens from village to village. Some travel on foot, others on bicycles. They leave their homes with baskets of chickens and traverse scores of miles, coming home several days later once they have sold their wares. Usually they make friends in many villages, since they have to spend several nights away from home.

One evening a hawker was caught without shelter. Dusk was falling fast and rain was threatening. He was in a village in which he had no friends, so he decided to hurry on to the next village a couple of miles away, where he was well-known. He had not covered a mile when rain started with tropical suddenness and intensity. He doubled back to the nearer village and sought refuge in the first compound with a light in it. He parked his bicycle in the reception hut and made for the door from which the light shone. A woman was cooking in the kitchen. She turned with a start at his greeting. The man explained his plight and asked to be allowed to spend the night in the reception hut. The woman recognized him vaguely as one of the hawkers who often passed through the village, and she let him stay. She sent one of her children to make a log fire in the reception hut to keep him and his chickens warm and comfortable. Later the woman sent the man a plate of food, which he accepted gratefully. This type of hospitality was quite usual.

After she had put her children to bed and bathed, the woman came to retrieve the plates. She had tied her wrapper just over her breasts, and her shoulders were bare. The man took a closer look at her and inquired after her husband. She said she was a widow. Then he made overtures. No, she said. What would her neighbours and relatives-in-law think of her? The man offered her a chicken. She laughed. She would rather have nothing than a chicken. The man did not miss the hint. He offered two chickens. Still the women demurred. By the time the offer had risen to three chickens they were inside her house. What the man needed, she said, was a warm room to sleep in, not someone to sleep with. He should therefore sleep in the empty room adjoining the bedroom. The man offered four chickens. At five chickens they were inside her bedroom. At six on the bed. At seven they were making love, but yet the bargaining went on. When, at the critical moment, the woman threatened to terminate his pleasure, the love-sick man, no longer in control, offered his entire basket of chickens. With the morning came sober reflections and regrets. The man, in desperation, tried to renegotiate terms. To his relief, the woman refused to accept any chickens and explained that she had been joking. The couple later got married.

This is the feminine sexual power which men fear. The women who oppose the feminist movement are mostly those who recognize this power. If the complete emancipation of women is to become a reality, maybe women should be ready to restrict the use of their sexual power as men are persuaded to moderate the exercise of their muscular superiority.

Good education may provide an answer – education in the art of living, that is. It is strange that although we teach our children all the subjects that should enable them to live, the art of living itself is never taught. Perhaps it is because we are apt to confuse the art of living with ideology and ideology with brainwashing. Rather than risk the last, we abandon this aspect of education. But we cannot dodge the issue indefinitely. In a few thousand years man has made the leap from the cave-dweller to the moon explorer, with all the social, mental and emotional adjustments that are involved. Now, from all indications the

Earth may remain habitable for a couple of million years. If mankind is to cope with the strains of unbroken progress during the course of such a long future, the sexes must endeavour to master the art of harmonious living as precisely as they are mastering the sciences.

Chapter 10

Awuf

He who drinks from a twisted horn arrives at twisted decisions.
(Ikwerre proverb)

In pidgin English (which is the unofficial *lingua franca* of Nigeria) *awuf* means bribery, corruption or any gain obtained through trickery, dishonesty or sharp practice. In pre-colonial Nigeria the areas in which *awuf* could be practised were severely limited. The one important area was the settlement of disputes. In most parts of the country, if a man was vexed by another and wanted a settlement, he usually summoned the offender to appear before the king, the council of elders or a powerful secret society, like the Ogboni among the Yoruba or the Ekpo among the Efik and Ibibio. Since the various secret societies were drawn from the populace, it was unlikely that their methods of judgement differed markedly from those commonly employed by the elders.

If a man sought justice among the Ikwerre, he would so inform the chief or elder of the village by paying one or two manillas as a summons fee. The other party would also be informed and would be expected to deposit an amount exactly equal to the summons fee paid by his opponent. The council of elders would be summoned on the appointed day, and the litigants would be called to state their cases, starting with the complainant. Any villager who wished could attend the hearing, which was never conducted in secret. Usually both parties would come along with their friends and relations for moral support. When the litigants had stated their cases they were allowed to ask each other questions. After that the elders also asked questions. If the answer to a particular question was disputed, and if it could affect the verdict, proceedings would be temporarily suspended and that question would be made the subject of a sub-inquiry, during which both parties would be asked to stake money on the veracity of their assertions. This stake, known as *mbawu* in Ikwerre and *ebe* in Igbo, was an important element in the judicial system of these tribes. Whoever was proved a liar lost his money on the side bet, and the main case was resumed. After the case had been thoroughly examined, the elders withdrew, out of earshot, for consultations which could last from a few minutes to several hours. When the elders eventually returned, the quarrelling parties were asked to produce either a bottle of gin each or money for the pronouncement of the verdict. Thereafter an elder, especially appointed for the occasion, announced the verdict. After every important pronouncement he would ask the council for confirmation, which was given by a general affirmation. Whoever lost the case lost the summons fee, which, along with drinks, was shared by the elders. Sometimes fines were levied or one party was asked to pay compensation to the other.

It was possible for an elder to receive money or drinks in order to further the cause of a particular litigant. During the consultations preceding the judgement that elder would argue ably in defence of his client, but his influence was quite limited. If a matter was clearly defined by tradition, there was usually little or no room to manoeuvre. In many ways the elder who received money to defend a litigant was the forerunner of the modern lawyer. Nzimiro refers to this practice in *Studies in Ibo Political Systems*. He recognizes four different payments made by litigants: the summons fee paid by the plaintiff; the 'answering' fee paid by the defendant; the sitting fee; and

> a fourth charge known as *ogo nde oka okwu*, the fee which a client pays separately to special 'local barrister' (*nde oka okwu*) who can be hired in this manner to come to court to plead his case. This is, however, a private arrangement between the client and the man who pleads for him.[1]

However one may choose to look at it, there was a hint of bribery in this practice, because the hired defender was also usually a member of the jury that gave the final verdict. Although a rich litigant could give money to more than one 'advocate', he could never buy over the entire council of elders, since his opponent had the right to choose some of the judges or elders to sit on the case. If a litigant had no relations or powerful friends within the village, he could invite elders and friends from other villages to sit in judgement. It was a right that could not be denied. Whenever the evidence was inadequate to support a clear and impartial judgement, especially in land disputes, recourse was made to the gods. One party was asked to swear by any god that the other party might choose. A time limit, usually one year, was set. If the swearer survived, he was vindicated; if he died, his opponent was in the right. In land disputes it was possible for a rich litigant to buy over many false witnesses, but the system had safeguards against this fraud. In serious cases all witnesses testified on oath. Usually this practice eliminated all false witnesses, for no one would swear if he knew he was going to tell a deliberate lie, so powerful was the fear of the gods. Furthermore, even if one party was able to produce an overwhelming number of witnesses, the other party still had the right to demand a trial by swearing.

Not all cases were brought before the council of elders. In minor disagreements a complainant might summon an offender to appear before just one elder. Usually the elder would ask the parties to bring along persons to assist him to arrive at a judgement. The gods were not usually invoked in such trivial cases, and *awuf* could well have been used to influence judgement, but usually there was not enough at stake to make *awuf* necessary.

Cases of the individual versus the tribe were usually very serious. They often had to do with abominations or with treason committed against the village, and usually they carried capital punishment. Such crimes included giving information to an enemy, witchcraft, the desecration of a shrine, murder and so on. In these cases powerful witnesses and eloquent advocates were particularly important. However, witnesses were not constrained to testify on oath. There were two reasons for this: first, the judges would not want to appear eager to do the defendant harm; second, there was the convention that a man fighting for his life should be given every possible chance of escape. However, it was believed that an offence committed against the village was, in fact, an offence against the Earth-god of the village. Thus false witnesses, whether or not they testified under oath, ran the grave risk of inviting the anger of the Earth-god. So although *awuf* was possible, it was minimal and not usually very effective.

Priests could also try cases directly. They enlisted elderly men as assistants, and the procedure was the same, except that the hearing was held in the shrine or close to the shrine, and the litigants were generally very conscious of being in the presence of a deity. Lying and *awuf* were almost completely eliminated. As a result, trials of non-criminal palavers by traditional priests have grown more and more popular over the years in Ikwerre and in other parts of eastern Nigeria. Operating very successfully now are many traditional priests, some of them sufficiently well-educated to keep a clear and accurate record of their judgements. Examples are the priest of Alakikia in Emohua, and that of Amadioha in

Ozuzu, both in the Rivers State. A few of them are corrupt, but these rapidly lose their reputation and their clients.

The Ikwerre judicial system has been described in some detail because investigations have revealed that the systems of the Igbo, the Efik, the Ibibio, the Ijaw and other eastern tribes are very similar. In general one can say that in these systems *awuf*, though it existed, had very little effect on the impartiality of judgement, thanks largely to the people's fear of the gods. On the effect of *awuf* on judgement Talbot has this to say:

> Though bribery was universal and considered to be more or less permissible, yet on the whole it seems probable that justice was fairly evenly administered. Since the cases were tried in public, bias would have been at once evident and would not have been tolerated by the people, any of whom might have suffered later in the same way.[2]

Among the Yoruba judicial proceedings at the lower level (that is, within compounds and families) were much the same as in eastern Nigeria. However, in the higher courts, where the Obas presided, there were notable differences. In the first place, the Oba chose his advisers, who were more or less permanently present in his court. Thus litigants had scarcely any rights in the choice of the jury, so to speak. This is a serious departure from what obtained in the east. In the second place, the Oba was not obliged to try cases in public. Even when trials were open to the general public, it was not easy for the ordinary man in the street to enter an Oba's palace merely to listen to a trial. In these circumstances *awuf* would appear to have had greater opportunity to flourish. Members of the jury could be bribed. Again, if the Oba himself was amenable to *awuf*, impartial decisions became even more chancey. But there were mitigating factors. For instance, a party to a dispute could always elect to be tried by ordeal. In *The Sociology of the Yoruba* Fadipe summarizes the effect of *awuf* as follows:

> The acceptance of gifts of money from parties in trouble with a view to obtaining leniency was not considered reprehensible. Rather, it was looked upon by the authorities as a legitimate source of revenue. The unfortunate party was bled right and left by the chiefs. After he had satisfied one, another was pointed out to him as worth cultivating. . . . However, these gifts to members of a judicial tribunal very rarely led to the guilty party being adjudged the

winner in case of a dispute between two parties. But it led to the
party in the right getting less than he would have got if strict justice
had been done to him. He was asked to make concessions. In this
respect the claim of seniority was sometimes invoked in favour of the
party with less right on its side.[3]

In northern Nigeria Islamic law prevailed in tribes that had been
converted to that religion. According to Michael Crowder: 'In the Habe
kingdoms, *gaisuwa*, or the giving of bribes to superiors, was common;
judges were open to bribery.'[4] And among the Nupe, 'the feudal lords
could be influenced in favour of a better-paying claimant, or prevented
by bribes from reporting a particular case [to the king].'[5] Still, *awuf* on a
large scale seems to have been kept at bay by the fear of Allah. Indeed,
until very recently the word of the northern Muslim was said to be his
bond. Whenever a dispute arose between a northern Muslim and any
other Nigerian, the former was almost always presumed to be telling the
truth. In recent years the northern Muslim has lost much of his
reputation in this regard because of the rough-and-tumble of the
socio-economic struggle. He can now call on Allah or swear by the
Koran nearly as glibly as the Christian invokes God and the Bible.

The so-called heathen north had a judicial system similar to that of the
southern tribes; that is to say, the elders of the tribe tried cases in open
court. When doubts could not be resolved, trial by ordeal was often
resorted to, perhaps more frequently than in the south. The ordeals were
more varied and included the ordeal of the saaswood poison, running the
tongue over a sharp knife, pulling a piece of iron from a pot of boiling
water, pouring boiling oil on the hands, passing a needle through the
tongue or ear lobe, pouring poisonous fluids into the eyes, jumping
repeatedly over a human skull, and so on. The result of an ordeal could
sometimes be manipulated through the influence of *awuf*. Thus a poison
brew for an ordeal could be diluted or strengthened. For instance, it was
known that saaswood poison could be made more potent by the addition
of salt. According to Temple:

> A very healthy person will nearly always throw it up unless salt has
> been added, which makes it more deadly. The Sarkin Gwaska,
> therefore, puts salt under his nails, and could thus introduce it unto
> the brew should he consider the death of the accused desirable.[6]

Talbot, commenting on the same issue with reference to southern tribes,
writes:

It is said that an overdose—or a previous boiling in the case of the (poisonous) bean—will always cause vomiting and that the doses were regulated by the priest according to whether the latter regarded the person as innocent or guilty—or, in some cases, whether he had been bribed or not. There can be little doubt that many of the ordeals were managed in this way, but it is probable that in the majority of cases the priest would fear the vengeance of the gods too much to cause the death of an innocent man.[7]

It is clear that religion has a very powerful influence over *awuf*. Many Nigerians lament the fact that the imported religions do not have the same effect as the indigenous religions. However, even the imported religions may be better than nothing, and this has led many to argue for the reintroduction of religious instruction in Nigerian public schools or, if that is not possible, the possibility of leaving the door open for religious groups who wish to establish private schools. But Nigeria is very wary of religious indoctrination, having observed its disintegrating effects in many parts of the world. The heyday of private mission schools may have gone for ever.

When the British took on the administration of Nigeria, the native judicial system was replaced by native courts. Although certain aspects of the native system, such as swearing by gods, were retained, it was clear that the natives did not respect the new system and did much to thwart it. Their scepticism was intensified by the fact that the warrant chiefs set up to administer the courts were often upstarts, and many were notoriously corrupt. (As we have noted, during the Aba women's riot of 1929, the women directed much of their anger against the warrant chiefs.) Also the warrant chiefs, court clerks and messengers who served the colonial administration saw the white man as a foolish intruder who should be outwitted at every possible opportunity. The effect of all this was to make the native courts notorious centres of *awuf*, in which everyone was out for what he could get. The natives thought they were sabotaging the white man, but they were, in fact, destroying the moral fabric of their own society. Although Nigeria became independent in 1960, a Civil Service appointment is still regarded by some as a white man's job, in which it is acceptable to cheat. C. K. Meek, writing in 1931, says in *A Sudanese Kingdom*:

Native courts are necessary under present conditions, but they should be used, as far as possible, as courts of appeal for the trial of exceptional cases, and always in close conjunction with the indigenous system of government. Otherwise the court is likely to prove one of the speediest methods of disrupting the tribal life.[8]

The influence of *awuf* can therefore be said to have taken a gigantic stride with the establishment of the native courts. Even today it is hard to say that the law courts in Nigeria, especially the lower ones, are completely free from bribery.

Along with the native courts, the British colonial rulers set up a Civil Service. It must be said that this is one of their greatest legacies to Nigeria. In its early days the Civil Service was almost immune from *awuf*. British officials, many of them excellent administrators, who manned the key posts saw to it that *awuf* was reduced to the barest minimum. As the British officials were gradually replaced by Nigerians, the incidence of *awuf* increased. One might be led to the conclusion that the British officials were of a higher moral and administrative calibre than their Nigerian counterparts. This is not necessarily so, but it is true that the white civil servants who were sent to Nigeria were very carefully screened and chosen and so made an efficient corps of dedicated public servants. Amaury Talbot, whose works have been quoted so frequently and so copiously in this book, was one of such administrators.

Today *awuf* exists in the Nigerian Civil Service. It must be said at once that many other countries around the world are in the same unhappy position, but that fact cannot serve as an excuse. Some Treasury clerks routinely demand bribes from contractors before paying them money duly approved by government for contracts properly executed; time-keepers demand *awuf* to mark even diligent labourers present; head labourers take *awuf* to protect workers absent from duty; messengers receive tips from members of the public in order to trace files dealing with their affairs; clerks demand *awuf* before they will give out supposedly free scholarship or employment forms to members of the public. Under the influence of *awuf*, tax officials reduce tax assessments; customs officials connive at the trafficking of contraband goods; recruitment officers ignore qualified candidates and recommend poorly qualified ones; top civil servants inflate contract figures and arrange for the balance to be paid into their bank accounts overseas; airways officials ignore passengers with confirmed tickets and give boarding passes even to those without tickets but with well-stocked wallets. School Certificate examination questions set by the West African Examinations Council leak as a matter of routine, as the Council workers and some unscrupulous headmasters of secondary schools simply cannot resist the temptation to make money by selling the question papers. At the universities admissions are sometimes made for reasons other than academic ones. The Joint Admissions and Matriculation Board was set up to cure this disease, but even this august body is considered by some to be not completely impregnable. When a dull female student achieves a first in her degree examinations, her success may not be attributable to a sudden upsurge of intellect. A driver can ignore all traffic rules because he can nearly always get away with it by offering *awuf*. For the same reason, a complainant can become the accused at a police station.

The saying 'Politics is a dirty game' is one which most politicians bandy about almost with glee. They are right; politics in Nigeria, as elsewhere, is a very dirty game. Voters must be bribed with money, drinks and goat meat. Politicians have been known to distribute money right at the voting line. To pay for the huge debts they accumulate during elections, many politicians make mincemeat of government treasuries as soon as they come to power; many contracts are inflated, and the commissioner or minister bags the extra.

Awuf assumes many guises. The popular form is, of course, money, but it may come as a free house, a car or some other material gift. It may take the form of a trading concession to a politician's company or sex.

The above picture looks grim, and one may wonder how Nigeria functions at all. The explanation is that, fortunately, *awuf* is still the exception rather than the rule. There are magistrates, judges, civil servants, policemen, university workers, public servants and politicians who resist corruption and try to do a fine job. If this were not the case, the country would have collapsed a long time ago. The Federal and State governments of Nigeria are very much aware of the evils of *awuf*, and they are waging a relentless war against it. The current Constitution embodies a code of conduct for all public servants, including a provision for the declaration of assets before accepting a public office and at the end of it. This code forms the Fifth Schedule to the Constitution. Paragraph 6 of the Schedule deals specifically with *awuf* and provides as follows:

> 6 (1) A public officer shall not ask for or accept any property or benefits of any kind for himself or any other person on account of anything done or omitted to be done by him in the discharge of his duties.
>
> (2) For the purposes of sub-paragraph (1) of this paragraph, the

receipt by a public officer of any gifts or benefits from commercial firms, business enterprises or persons who have contracts with the government shall be presumed to have been received in contravention of the said sub-paragraph unless the contrary is proved.

(3) A public officer shall only accept personal gifts or benefits from relatives or personal friends to such extent and on such occasions as are recognized by custom: provided that any gift or donation to a public officer on any public or ceremonial occasion shall be treated as a gift to the appropriate institution represented by the public officer, and accordingly, the mere acceptance or receipt of any such gift shall not be treated as a contravention of this provision.

These provisions are worthwhile, but their effect on the moral tone of the nation remains to be seen.

What is the attitude of Nigerians to *awuf*? To begin with, everyone agrees, even if vaguely, that *awuf* is not in the best interests of the nation. But some people are not prepared to do anything about it because they believe that it cannot be eradicated. It is foolish, they claim, not to join in the game.

Then there are those who think that life is a grim battle for survival. Quite a few buses bear the inscription 'Life is War'. For those who believe this, it is a waste of time to talk of morality. The important thing is to have enough bread to feed yourself and your children. People in this group merely smile when they come across cases of *awuf* and wish themselves in the shoes of the lucky '*awuf*-eater'.

Another group, and it is a fairly large one, believes that a bargain is a bargain, and that as long as one performs the task for which one has received *awuf*, one's conscience should be clear. After all, no one is forced to give *awuf*. But this is not true, for often citizens find they desperately need one form of public service or another, and if the public servants who are paid to render the service refuse to do so, then the citizen may well be forced to pay *awuf*. The sick person who requires urgent medical attention provides a ready example. If the doctor refuses to attend to him until he is paid a bribe, then the patient has no choice but to do so. In fact, every case of *awuf* amounts to criminal extortion.

Another group may be described as the passive operators. They argue that if a member of the public voluntarily offers gifts in acknowledgement of services rendered, then the receiver cannot be blamed. A magistrate interviewed on the matter stated quite frankly that he never asked for *awuf* before a judgement, but that if a litigant felt grateful after receiving a favourable judgement and offered him money, he never refused it. Gratitude, he said, was a natural impulse; to spurn a grateful person showed poor manners. He disagreed with the suggestion that the expectation of a handsome reward from a rich litigant could affect his judgement. The law, he said, was straightforward, and judgement was given strictly according to the law. When it was pointed out to him that since judgement was, as he claimed, given strictly according to the law, he had no grounds for claiming any litigant's gratitude, he shrugged and complained of a poor salary.

Many businessmen laugh when the subject of *awuf* is raised. *Awuf*, they say, is just a way of being nice to people. They claim that the business world is very different from the world of, say, public service; that in business it is of the utmost importance to maintain good public relations, and this cannot be done with empty hands. They refuse to draw any line between a gift and an *awuf*. If one wants to win a big contract, then one could be nice to the people who are in a position to award it. One businessman interviewed on the matter said that the presentation of gifts was a way of showing respect, and that refusing to give gifts could amount to disregard of, or even an insult to, one's business associates. He drew attention to the Nigerian tradition of offering cola and drinks to a person before opening an important discussion. *Awuf* is nothing but cola, he said. It was pointed out to him that if, for example, he gave expensive cola to a government official in order to get a contract, then the price of the contract would have to go up, in which case the taxpayer would have to pay more than was necessary and this would be ethically wrong. His reply was that he was not responsible for the system, and that companies were put in a position where they either had to offer bribes for contracts or face liquidation, with its attendant unemployment for many people. Admittedly, business houses are sometimes held to ransom by avaricious public officers, and they collude with them to avoid facing the grim prospects of liquidation. But it is also true that even when an impartial system has been set up for the award of contracts, businessmen eager to put their competitors at a disadvantage pressurize public servants to accept *awuf* and so thwart the system. Could not private companies form a union and put up a common front against corruption? Every businessman interviewed said emphatically that such an idea was impracticable.

Whatever may be the case, it is wrong to equate *awuf* with the Nigerian cola and drinks. The latter do not vary according to circumstance and usually amount to very little when reckoned in terms of money. Even with current inflation, a large piece of cola costs ten kobo and a bottle of native gin about one naira. *Awuf*, on the other hand, escalates in proportion to the favour requested.

Nigerian intellectuals are rather unpredictable in their attitudes to *awuf*. Often they decry it vehemently when they are not in a position to play the game. When they acquire positions of power, they usually pipe down and rationalize. The professor who also is a food contractor to his university is not unknown. He argues that this is business, not *awuf*. He renders a service in his private time and gets paid. But then he overlooks the fact that one of his conditions of employment is that he should not engage in any other business while in the full employ of the university.

Then there are those who vehemently oppose *awuf* and propose a number of solutions to the problem. One solution is the establishment of codes of conduct for not only public servants but also professionals in private practice. As already pointed out, the code of conduct for public officials is embodied in the Constitution. Many professions, like the medical and the legal, have drawn up strict codes of conduct. But codes of conduct do not work nearly as well as they should because the two parties to an *awuf* transaction have a stake in the matter and, being usually the only witnesses, can hardly be expected to expose themselves if the deal works out.

There is the proposition that careful education, incorporating moral instruction, may help. The trouble here is that even at school students are brought up to appreciate *awuf*. A student's father may bribe the headmaster for admission and may pay the class teacher for extra lessons for his child – and all this is known to the child. The student himself buys leaked question papers and does his best to cheat at examinations. Thus by the time he has left school he should be well-versed in *awuf*. For him it has become the norm. So our education does not liberate the young from *awuf* but steeps them in it. Education will help only when teachers acquire higher moral standards; but they have little incentive to do this because already a vicious circle has been set in motion. The corrupt teacher brings up corrupt students, who in turn become corrupt teachers.

Some people hope that corruption will cease as soon as the nation achieves a higher living standard, since most people steal public funds or demand *awuf* in order to buy expensive cars, to build and furnish their houses and to send their children to school. If government is able eventually to satisfy most of these desires, then *awuf* and other forms of corruption should become less widespread. We have only to look at nations with high standards of living to realize that this argument is not wholly tenable. In these countries *awuf* and other vices still abound.

Yet others advocate religion as a panacea. A strong belief in God and adherence to religious principles should solve the problem they say. Cynics point out that Christianity was introduced into Nigeria about a century ago and that, if anything, immorality has been on the increase since then.

Then there is the communist argument. *Awuf* and other vices, it is said, are a direct result of the craving for property; communism, therefore, should eliminate *awuf*. It is true that in communist countries the desire to steal on a large scale is less pronounced because the thief who steals anything considerable cannot use his stolen property. As if to compensate, petty pilfering goes on all the time. The petrol attendant gives extra rations if offered *awuf*, and the public taxi driver still expects a tip.[9] However, the main drawback of communism is the severe curtailment of human freedom.

What then? Will no remedy work? Well, the remedies discussed above are not entirely without merit. They should be applied in the hope that in the very long run they will pay off. But the responsibility for ridding the nation of *awuf*, at least on a large scale, rests on intellectuals, thinkers, philosophers and administrators. They should endeavour to evolve a philosophical system to deal with the ills of the nation. In order to succeed in this, they themselves must keep as clear of those ills as possible and must present the nation with a new set of values. One reason why Nigeria did not break up at the time of the Civil War was because everyone preached unity relentlessly. It became an obsession; disunity was identified as public enemy number one. Today one can say confidently that Nigeria is very unlikely to break up. In much the same way *awuf* could be eradicated by relentless attacks.

Chapter 11

Leadership

*Those who take a decision behind a strong man's back may have to meet
again on the issue.*   (Ikwerre proverb)

Leadership always carries power with it. The proper exercise of power
always involves ethical considerations. In this chapter we shall examine
to what extent such ethical considerations have influenced Nigerian
leaders.

In pre-colonial Nigeria there were two main types of government
– monarchy and a democratic form of gerontocracy. The former featured
in kingdoms ruled by Obas, Emirs, Obongs, Obis and powerful tribal
chieftains, who wielded power in styles ranging from absolute
dictatorship to near-democracy. Democratic gerontocracy was found
typically among the Igbo and their neighbours, and we shall examine it
first.

Among the Ikwerre, who share a common boundary with the Igbo,
there were no kings whose status was comparable with, say, that of the
Oba of Benin. Villages and communities were governed by councils of
elders. The most senior of the elders was usually the head of the
community. Sometimes he was also the priest of the Earth-god, but such
a situation was the exception rather than the rule. Although he was
known as Eze (king), he could not take arbitrary decisions without full
consultations with the councils of elders. The rest of the community did
not minister to him. He had his farm and ran his affairs like any other
villager. When the villagers worked for him they did so voluntarily and
in recognition of his services to the community.

There were, once in a while, a few powerful Ezes who tried to wield
more power than was traditionally allowed them, but such rulers did not
last long. They could be accused of witchcraft, for instance, and, with the
assistance of Aro agents, sold into slavery. However, the real restraints
on rulers were religious. Even when a ruler was not a priest, he still had
many rituals to perform. These rituals had tabus which the ruler would
not dare to infringe. The Ikwerre Eze kept the Great Horn of the

community from which he poured libations. (A libation is an offering of drinks to the gods accompanied by poetic affirmations of justice and fair play and an invocation to the gods to enforce these concepts.) Now, the Eze would not offer libations if he were afflicted by a guilty conscience, for the gods would strike him dead. Thus if he was involved in a dispute with any citizen, he had to settle it amicably and quickly. If summoned to the council of elders for that purpose, he had to appear, just as every other citizen did, and was obliged to comply with any judgement arrived at. Although it might seem that the system weakened the power of the Eze, the contrary was, in fact, the case. Because he too was subject to the law, it was almost unthinkable for anyone to dispute any ruling arrived at by a council of elders, especially when the Eze presided. Thus he had very great moral authority over the people. If an Eze committed a serious offence – and this was rare – he was tried like anyone else and punished accordingly. It is true, however, that his influence could temper the punishment that was regarded as appropriate for that offence. For instance, if he committed murder, he might persuade the people to waive execution and to accept slaves as compensation. In this case he would still have to abdicate, since he could not rule with a 'bloody' hand. The Eze also kept the Owho (Ofo) sticks. These are symbols of justice and retribution. They also represent the twin gods Owho and Ogwu, who protect the innocent. Now, whoever kept these symbols was required at all times and within human limits to have a clear conscience or face the terrible anger of the gods. These restraints on the Eze forced him to live a good life and made him semi-divine. His curse, which he very rarely used, was regarded as fatal.

During a war the Eze, if he was not too old, was expected to lead his people in battle. He assumed the role of a general. In return he received the lion's share of the spoils of battle, usually prisoners-of-war who were sold off as slaves.

If the Eze was rich, he would have many wives, a number of them pawns who could not be redeemed by their parents. As there was much to be gained from having the Eze as an in-law, many a man borrowed money from the Eze and pawned his daughter without any intention of redeeming her. After a set time limit the Eze would formally marry the girl or else turn her over to one of his sons. Otherwise the Eze could not appropriate any woman without the due process of marriage.

The Igbo had a similar system and have been described as a very democratic people. V. C. Uchendu summarizes Igbo leadership thus: 'In translating the power relations in Igbo society into status terms, it is

more appropriate to speak of leaders and their supporters rather than of
rulers and their subjects.'[1] In *Niger Ibos* Basden quotes the proverb *Ibo
enwero eze* ('The Ibos have no king'). He goes on:

> In times of emergency a dominating character automatically came
> to the front, and the people accepted him as leader until the trouble
> ceased. He then reverted to his former position in common with
> other citizens. Nor were any hereditary rights attached to the
> erstwhile leadership; the basic principle of no ruling families in
> Iboland remained inviolate. Where such prerogatives are
> beginning to appear, they are the fruit of modern innovations; they
> are really contraventions of native laws and customs.[2]

Nzimiro quite rightly challenges the view that the Igbo had no kings. In
the preface to *Studies in Ibo Political Systems* he writes:

> There is a widespread belief that Ibo societies are acephalous. This
> belief does not take into account the differences between cultural
> areas revealed by Forde and Jones. Hence it has loomed in the
> minds of some social anthropologists that all Ibo cultural groups fall
> within this classificatory type, in which case the belief becomes a
> misconception.[3]

The Onitsha Igbo, who have a secure and long-standing monarchy,
lend support to Nzimiro's contention. The case of Onitsha is not
surprising, since it has been established that these people came from
Benin, where powerful Obas had held sway for centuries. Indeed, until
fairly recently the Onitsha people did not regard themselves as Igbo, and
they took offence if addressed as such. The Obi of Onitsha ruled through
a hierarchy, with a prime minister and a council of elders.

As if to make up for the scarcity of kings, the Igbo had a long catalogue
of titles, the highest being the Ozo and Ogbuefi (or Ogbu-inyinya), titles
which carried tremendous respect. According to Edmund Ilogu:

> The privileges which the Ozo man enjoys are many but the
> principal ones relate to political and social status. In most Ibo areas
> only the Ozo men hold political offices and represent their families
> and lineages in the village group councils or preside over settlement
> of cases, making of covenants, and the establishment of new cults.
> Socially they belong to the nobleman's rank – a social status marked

out by the honour accorded to those holding that position. They also take precedence in all public entertainments and feasts, irrespective of their age. For instance, at Onitsha the Ozo man, however young, is to be served first at public meals; he alone can carry and blow the elephant tusk, put eagle feathers on his cap, sit on a goat's skin on the dais, pour libations of wine to the spirits of dead ancestors. . . . He is exempt from menial manual labour.[4]

Some very poor people were known to have pawned their land and belongings to acquire the title. Thus the highest honour in the land was accessible to all. Because of this the Igbo have been regarded as among the most democratic and egalitarian tribes in Nigera.

Since the high titles were available to all who could pay for them, it would appear that respect and dignity could be purchased. Thus at first sight status and influence would appear to have been influenced by economic rather than moral considerations. One could be led to conclude that the Igbo society was a materialistic one, in which money meant everything. That would be a hasty and false conclusion. People were also honoured for brave deeds and for their devotion to justice. An elder who persistently spoke the truth and delivered impartial judgements won much respect among the people, even though he gained nothing material. Time and age were important yardsticks in determining the hierarchy of respect. An older man almost always took precedence over a younger man in, say, the council of elders, other things being equal. Among title-holders the order of precedence was determined strictly by the chronological order in which titles were conferred. Since time is a neutral yardstick, it helped the Igbo to maintain their democratic gerontocracy.

As with the Ikwerre, religion imposed a healthy restraint on Igbo leadership. The symbols of justice were respected, and belief in retributive justice was strong. Famous gods such as Chukwu of Arochukwu and Igwekala of Umunoha inspired the necessary fear and reverence in the people.

South of Igbo country live the Ijaw, who had a well-established system of chiefs and kings. There were the Amanyanabos and famous Delta kings like Jaja of Opobo, Nana of Itsekiri and Boy of Brass. Succession was hereditary or confined to a few ruling families. The administrative system was generally feudal. The kings had a large number of slaves, who, in the company of the freeborn, fished and traded for the king; in turn the king looked after them. According to Talbot;

One of the first duties of a chief was to look after and protect all the members of his 'house'. Such a case as that of a man dying of starvation was unknown. However this feudalism was not through-going.[5]

Again to quote Talbot:

Among all Ijaw the authority of the chiefs was kept in check by the Council of the old men or by the Sakapu Club, which amongst some peoples, such as the Kalabari proper, held the chief power and really administered the country.[6]

East of the Igbo are the Efik and Ibibio. Each of their towns and communities was ruled by a king known as Obong. The most outstanding was the Obong of Calabar. Here again, councils of elders greatly assisted the kings to rule their people.

Crossing the Niger westwards, we come to a country of formerly powerful kings. There were the Obis of Agbor, Ogwashi Uku and Aboh and, further west, the great Oba of Benin, who ruled a state that historians concur in regarding as the most powerful on the West African coast from the fifteenth century until the colonial era. Under Oba Owuare the Benin empire was said to have extended as far west as the Niger.[7] Because of the vast size of his empire, the Oba had to call on numerous chiefs and princes to rule various portions of it. Within Benin itself he had his prime minister, the Iyase, and the Uzama or king-makers, who advised him. However, there can be no doubt that the Oba wielded almost absolute power.

The Oba of Benin had a large number of tabus to observe and rituals to perform, and it is certain, to judge from the general trend, that some of them were designed to ensure good moral behaviour. Details of the personal lives of the ancient Obas are hard to come by and even more difficult to authenticate when obtained, but nearly all historical accounts of Benin point to one moral lapse, namely, the propensity for human sacrifice. In ancient Nigeria human sacrifice was commonplace, and Benin was probably no worse in this respect than other kingdoms of comparable size and power; however, because she was a historical focal point, the searchlights of history were beamed on her and consequently both her greatness and her lapses appeared in bold relief. As the Benin empire was a great slave centre controlled by the Oba, slaves for sacrifice must have been all too easy to obtain. No doubt many of the sacrifices were connected with religious matters and could not have been avoided, but there is little doubt that the Oba could have reduced the number of sacrifices drastically if he had so desired. The British found in this practice a very good excuse for invading the Benin empire. Since British motives were largely mercenary and guided by self-interest, it is possible – indeed, probable – that their accounts of human sacrifice in Benin were exaggerated.

Moving further west, we come to Yoruba country. Here again, we have a splendid array of famous and powerful kings. There were the great Alafin of Oyo, the Oni of Ife, the Alake of Abeokuta, the Awujale of Ijebu, the Owa of Ijesha. They all wielded considerable power. According to the Reverend Samuel Johnson: 'The government of Yoruba Proper is an absolute monarchy; the king is more dreaded than even the gods.'[8]

How did the possession of this vast power affect the behaviour of these leaders? The Obas, chiefs and family heads certainly looked after their subjects. They considered it their moral responsibility to do so. In return, they demanded and obtained certain privileges. For instance, according to Afolabi Ojo:

A hunter presented to the Oba the following parts of an animal whenever and wherever killed: the skin of a leopard, the tail and ivory of the elephant, and the tail feather of the egret. In exchange he received the apparels worn by the Oba when the presentation was made.[9]

Naturally, the Obas guarded their supremacy very jealously. No one within their kingdom was allowed to rival them in prestige or pomp. Afolabi Ojo records a rather amusing instance of this insistence on supremacy:

The Alafin of Oyo prevented his townspeople for some time from replacing the grass-thatched roofs of their houses with corrugated iron in order not to detract from the distinction of his palace which had been so treated. In Lagos a man was put to death with great cruelty after his goods had been confiscated for erecting a house similar to that of the Oba.[10]

And at Oguta

it is forbidden for anyone to wear any dress which is red in colour, for red robes are part of the regalia of kingship and can only be worn by the Obi, the Iyase, the Ezeukwu, the Ndanike and the Ezekoro.[11]

Proceeding northwards, we come to the country of the Emirs. The Emirs were powerful feudal lords. There were the Emir of Kano, the Emir of Zaria, the Shehu of Bornu, Etsu Nupe, Sultan of Sokoto, and many more. Wherever kings did not exist in the north, government was by councils of elders, not unlike those that we find in the south. For our study of a typical northern king, we shall focus on the Jukun kingdom, which was an absolute monarchy, but here again we find serious attempts to bind him with the usual religious shackles.

> The absolute power of the king is curtailed by the necessity of living in accord with the priest of the more important cults, especially those priests who have charge of parts of the bodies of former kings. For . . . a priest who has charge of the skull or hands of a former king has only to threaten to expose these sacred relics in order to compel the king to toe the line. The exposure of the relics would cause the king to sicken and die. . . . The king or chief was, in fact, at the mercy of his ancestors.[12]

In spite of these restraints, the king of the Jukun wielded considerable authority.

> The king is supreme. His decisions have a divine authority, and there is no appeal. Before the advent of the British government he had the power of life and death. . . . He could order the deposition or execution of chiefs. . . . He could command his people to till the royal fields and repair the palace. He could appropriate the major portion of all fines. . . . He claimed a share of all major game animals killed by hunters, and he exacted a penalty of seven slaves from any household a member of which had been responsible for causing a virgin girl to become enceinte. . . . He could take as a wife not merely any unmarried girl he pleased, but the wife of any of his subjects. If two suitors quarrelled over a girl, the king might settle the matter by appropriating the girl himself.[13]

These are awesome powers indeed; and it is clear that if the king chose, he could cast morality to the winds in certain matters and get away with it.

Like their pre-colonial ancestors, modern Nigerian rulers have their moral lapses. Moreover, they are exposed to greater temptation, since they supervise the wealth of larger chunks of the nation than those dominated by ancient tribal kings. Immorality often takes the form of the misappropriation of common funds. Contracts are inflated with the connivance of contractors, and the extra money is tucked away in banks overseas, usually Swiss banks, which are notorious for their intricate banking systems designed to camouflage financial transactions – and, as a consequence, international swindles. (Incidentally, it is surprising that the world banking community has never considered it necessary to establish and enforce a code of conduct that would discourage such unwholesome practices.) Another method that rulers employ to syphon off public funds is to allocate in the yearly budget large sums of money under items like 'contingency' or 'security' which the chief executives alone are empowered to spend, without reference to anyone else. Apart from money, modern Nigerian rulers also use their position to acquire houses and land.

Another common moral lapse is the tendency to distort justice. This happens when a prominent party member is involved in a criminal case. Since such cases are normally prosecuted by the Attorney-General, who is a political appointee, it is only too easy for cases to be withdrawn from court. The Attorney-General simply orders the Crown counsel to plead *nolle prosequi*. The matter dies, and the police are powerless to pursue it. Thus although magistrates and judges are not obstructed directly, politicians have very effective ways of thwarting justice.

A third moral lapse is nepotism, a topic that has been discussed in chapter 8. Powerful political rulers are particularly well-placed to ensure that their kinsmen are appointed to favourable jobs at the expense of other members of the public.

This quick survey of leadership has revealed interesting facts, which may be useful in explaining certain political tendencies in Nigeria. First, we have seen that in spite of the shackles of religion ancient Nigerian kings were monarchs who ruled until death. This aspect of our culture is probably responsible for the tendency of modern Nigerian rulers to attempt to remain in office through thick and thin. The idea of being a powerful ruler one day and a powerless man in the street the next is simply unbearable for those with a tradition of monarchy. In pre-war governments many Ministers of State were contemptuously referred to as 'sit-tight' ministers because nothing could induce them to quit office, not even a vote of no confidence, a nationwide scandal or evident public dissatisfaction with their administration. This is why the promise of a voluntary surrender of power by the military in Nigeria was never believed until it actually happened. It was a pleasant shock to many. (Incidentally, General Olusegun Obasanjo, the military ruler who relinquished power in October 1979, comes from the Yoruba tribe, a nation of great kings.)

The second observation one can make is that democracy was here long before the British came. What was unknown was the institution of loyal opposition in government. If any issue was in doubt, the council of elders debated the question until it arrived at an agreement. No person or group of people persistently opposed the common will merely for the sake of maintaining a 'balance' in the debate. If a matter was so obvious that it did not require debate, then there was no debate. In the light of this cultural background, it is not at all surprising that practically all Nigerian governments have found the institution of the opposition extremely difficult to accommodate. The ruling party has always harassed the opposition until it was impotent or dead. To avert such a calamity, some members of losing parties in an election often switched over to the winning party to grab what offices they could. Another peculiarly Nigerian solution to the problem has been for the ruling party and its major political opponent to come to an 'accord' or 'working agreement'.

But by comparison with other African states, Nigeria has tolerated the new concept of opposition fairly well. Many African nations have one-party systems headed by men who are virtually presidents for life. Some heads of state have been in the saddle for decades. They have briskly and systematically eliminated all opposition. In an African country where one major tribe outnumbers all others, the one-party system works, for the dominant tribe invariably forms the dominant party. Where there are two or more major tribes, as in Nigeria, Zaire, Uganda and Chad, trouble is always erupting. The Nigerian problem has been cleverly solved by chopping the country into states, each with a dominant or nearly dominant tribe. There are some states that are tribally homogeneous. In those states where no one tribe is overwhelmingly dominant, however, agitation for the creation of more states persists even now.

Is it possible to weld the traditional concepts of government into an instrument capable of coping with the running of a modern state? That is the possibility that African nations should explore. Unfortunately, most African countries are not doing this. Instead they are seeking ready answers from either the East or the West, thereby incurring the antagonism of whichever bloc they have rejected. But neither system can provide an answer to the African situation. Thoroughgoing communism destroys the cherished African tradition of possession of land and property. Capitalism ultimately vests the economy in the hands of the few rich and effectively dispossesses the individual, converting him into a mere workhorse chained to the whirling wheels of huge industrial machines.

Nigeria has recently taken as a model the American Constitution, which has some features that, one suspects, may well have attracted many Nigerians. A look at this Constitution reveals that it is an amalgam of certain Nigerian concepts. Those tribes with ancient monarchies may find in the executive President a kingly figure with considerable powers. The more democratic tribes will see in the Senate and the National Assembly a reflection of the village council of elders. But although opposition is not as fully institutionalized in the new Nigerian Constitution as it is in the British, it is there all the same, in spite of 'accords' and 'working agreements' among the parties. One way to eliminate, or at any rate to neutralize, destructive opposition is to make it possible for members of the Senate and National Assembly to vote according to conscience, if not on all issues, at least on national issues. Such a system would, no doubt, be difficult to adopt, since it would always be possible for parties to apply pressure to their members to vote in a particular way. Also it can be argued that since, at least in theory, parties are voted into power on the basis of their manifestos, it would be inconsistent for individual politicians not to adhere to those manifestos, and adhering to them entails voting according to the party's wishes much of the time. Another possible way of minimizing damaging opposition is for the President to appoint the members of his Cabinet from among all the parties in proportion to the votes that they gain at the polls. Thus the least popular party would have the smallest number of ministerial appointments. If all parties were involved in the government of the country to a greater or lesser extent, none could stand aloof as an opposition party. It might then be possible to persuade party members in the house to vote according to their conscience on all issues. The advantages of this system would be considerable. First, the majority party would be restrained from carrying out its more extreme policies. Second, the minority parties would always have a chance to contribute to the running of the government instead of lying fallow until they won an election. Third, elections would be less bitter and far less expensive.

One aspect of traditional Nigerian government which cannot be worked into the modern system is the religious aspect. For one thing, there are nearly as many religions as there are tribes; for another it is clear from what is happening in the religious nations of the world that religion in the hands of unscrupulous rulers becomes a weapon which can be wielded viciously, relentlessly and irrationally. But what substitute is there for the restraining effects of religion? It is difficult to see any. In my view, there can be none until man outgrows religion and leaps to the next stage of his intellectual evolution.

Chapter 12

Conclusion

If a man claims to have sung till dawn, find out when he started.

(Ikwerre proverb)

We have examined various aspects of life among some Nigerian tribes and have analysed their ethical content. There is no claim here to complete coverage of the subject, either in breadth or in depth, but perhaps enough has been said to give a general picture of Nigerian ethics.

Among the facts that stand out is the part played by religion in enforcing ethical precepts. It is doubtful whether religion, imported or native, can continue to play this role, for already it is apparent that fear of the gods is diminishing steadily. A substitute for religion which could have the same emotional appeal will be hard to find. Even humanism is inadequate. Yet something has to be done to support the legal system, for, as is well-known, there would be far more crime if fear of punishment were the only deterrent. Conscience and religion probably constrain criminal behaviour at least as much as the fear of punishment.

One possible solution is to reintroduce moral instruction into education, but not in the old, ineffectual manner. Moral instruction and ethical philosophy should be made compulsory subjects in schools and universities respectively. Teachers of ethics should be selected with the same discrimination as is now applied in recruiting candidates for the priesthood. They should be exemplary and dedicated men and women who live what they preach. They should be accorded the same honour in society as is now accorded to High Court judges. As soon as they fall short of the code of conduct to which they aspire, they should be removed from office. Under such a system society would have people to respect and emulate, whose lives would provide fine moral examples. In particular, right from the start the young would have proper guidance. It would be incorrect to argue that since goodness cannot be precisely defined, it would be impossible to draw up a syllabus for moral teaching. The problems of definition notwithstanding, it should not be too difficult to inculcate the principle that in general theft and murder are unethical. After all, the current Nigerian Constitution embodies codes of conduct. A syllabus for the teaching of morals would be nothing but a synthesis of all the codes of conduct of all professions. If the young demanded a reason for moral instruction, as some undoubtedly would, the simple answer would be that it is necessary for human happiness and survival. It should be pointed out that if murder were condoned, life would be most uncomfortable for everybody. When they matured, the young could work out their own reasons for good behaviour.

Along with ethical philosophy should be taught elementary metastronomy, which is here defined as a mixture of astronomy, philosophy and religion. This should give people an idea of the place of our planet Earth in the cosmological scheme and of the status of man in the universe. Such knowledge is bound to reduce drastically the geocentricity which encourages nations to go to war and the egocentricity whch leads individuals to commit crime. There is nothing Utopian about these suggestions. Once a good moral foundation has been laid in schools and universities, all unethical practices like discrimination, *awuf* and injustice will diminish considerably.

Another outstanding feature of the Nigerian ethical system is the strong feeling of kinship which results in the celebrated extended family. This practice should be studied in greater depth and worked into a political philosophy. The ultimate hope of all the peoples of the world is the realization of the universal brotherhood of man. Here in Nigeria that hope is already realized at the tribal and clan level. It should be nursed, expanded and made the basis of a Nigerian ideology.

The Nigerian government has accorded some recognition to the extended-family system by providing tax relief for workers who cater for dependents, provided the number of such dependents does not exceed two. This is token recognition. Government should now support the system boldly and should adopt it as a feature of its welfare scheme. It should provide generous tax relief for up to ten dependents, though it would be necessary, of course, to devise a fool-proof system of checking the existence of such dependents in order to eliminate false declarations.

At the moment government-subsidized housing ranges from one-bedroom to three-bedroom flats. In pursuance of the extended-family system, the range should be from three-bedroom flats to ten-bedroom super-flats, to be allocated to those who can show that they have many genuine dependents. The advantages of such a policy are obvious. There would be fewer beggars and homeless applicants roaming the streets, and there would be no need to build so many asylums and old people's homes. Every Nigerian home should be a haven for the old and the destitute. It may be argued that such a system would encourage laziness in dependants. The answer to that objection is that the experience gained from centuries of this practice indicates that the opposite is likely to be the case. No one is happy to be dependent on a relation for ever. In any case, the provider himself cannot last for ever; he will eventually grow old and become a dependant himself. This hard fact spurs everyone to struggle hard to stand on his own. Some may also argue that a well-planned welfare system would be just as good – perhaps better – than the grand extended-family ideology proposed here. This cannot be true. The extended-family system is based on love and duty, whereas the ordinary welfare system is based on duty alone. No nurse can look after a grandfather as well as his own children or relations. The nurse may be efficient, but she cannot provide the emotional background of love and security which the old and the infirm need.

Social clubs, which have grown out of two important traditional concepts, namely, the secret society and the extended-family system are a step in the right direction. They have several advantages over the two roots from which they have sprouted. First, they are not confined to particular families, clans or tribes but are open to all Nigerians who are prepared to abide by the rules. Second, the system of contributions and benefits is carefully spelt out; thus members know beforehand exactly what to expect. Third, the affairs of the clubs are conducted in the open, and they have none of the mysterious and suspicious rituals characteristic of secret societies. Fourth, in moments of crisis members receive not only material benefits but also solace, compassion and companionship which may well rival those of the extended-family system. The government should take off from here and organize all citizens into social clubs. This could be done quite easily through the various local governments. Such a system would ensure social security for all citizens in both material and emotional terms.

As for the institution of kingship, it should be preserved as long as people are willing to put up with it. It is a good thing that the present civilian regime has decided to do just that. Any attempt to end it abruptly would almost certainly generate unnecessary frustration and unrest. In our present stage of political evolution the Emirs, Obas, Obis Ezes, Obongs and Amanyanabos can still serve as useful agencies of administration and as cultural rallying points. Unfortunately, many of

these traditional rulers, in their desire to grow rich quickly and to keep
up with the times, have abandoned most of their moral scruples and have
taken to practices which tradition would not normally have condoned.
Thus they are gradually losing their moral authority over the people. If
this process goes on unchecked, their powers are bound to wane, just as
in Britain the barons, dukes and lords have lost much of the influence
they once commanded. Whatever the case, kingship has no future.

Sexual discrimination is an immoral practice which Nigerians should
examine closely. As already pointed out, Nigeria is a man's country, and
things ought to change considerably in favour of women. All the
disadvantages experienced by single women should vanish. No woman's
career should suffer because she has a baby. She should not only receive
full pay during her confinement, but she should also be paid a bonus to
help her nurse her baby. Schoolgirls should be properly informed about
how to avoid pregnancy, but if they do become pregnant, they should be
allowed to return to school after confinement, and no stigma should be
attached to such a situation. In having a baby a woman is playing a very
vital role in society, a role which has to do with the very survival of
mankind. It is the height of hypocrisy and irony that she should be
ridiculed or made to suffer any disability for playing that role. By paying
a bonus to a nursing mother, the government stands to gain. The mother
is better able to feed her child well and therefore to ensure its healthy
development. It has been scientifically established that the first five
years are crucial to the mental development of a child. Proper mental
development depends on good feeding. Society has nothing to gain, and
much to lose when a child becomes mentally retarded, for that child
ultimately swells the number of vagabonds roaming the streets and
plaguing society.

Prostitution is a practice for which women are hounded, prosecuted
and humiliated. Most women are driven to prostitution because they
have no other viable means of earning their living – usually because they
have been denied a good education or training in favour of their brothers.
A working woman cannot be a prostitute. She may have many male
friends, but that does not make her a prostitute. If it does, then the same
appellation should be applied to men who have many girlfriends. The
fact is that prostitutes exist only because there are men who patronize
them. It is hypocritical and unfair for men to condemn prostitutes
without at the same time condemning themselves. The classic definition
of a prostitute is a woman who demands money in exchange for sexual
intercourse. The general feeling is that the profit element of her

profession condemns her. But is a man who offers money for a woman's favours blameless? It is as if men feel that the payment of money absolves them from guilt, while it steeps women in sin. Any such feeling is clearly illogical.

The solution to prostitution does not lie in legislation either against it or in its favour, as in West Germany and other European countries. The solution lies in providing women with the same job opportunities as men and in catering for them while in confinement. Polygamy should not be abolished in Nigeria. Those men and women who can cope with that system of marriage should be allowed to contract it. Short-sighted feminists may regard this suggestion as unjust. They may feel that a women should hold her man fast and not share him with another woman. But if women consider the fact that right now they outnumber men in Nigeria, and that a woman in a happy polygamous marriage is in a far better position than a whore who is roaming the streets, a disgrace to womanhood, they will come to realize that in the circumstances polygamy is in their own interest. While women fight for equality with men, they should also endeavour to foster love among themselves, the love that makes polygamy workable. Some feminists argue that since polygamy is legally sanctioned, the same consideration should be given to polyandry. That argument is logical and valid. Polyandry is, in fact, practised in certain parts of the world (Tibet, for example). However, the fact that in Nigeria women outnumber men makes its wider application impracticable. But it must be admitted that in the final analysis male domination and patriarchy are the real obstacles to polyandry.

Finally, what about those concepts of goodness that are peculiar to Nigerians – the automatic invitation to a stranger to share a meal, the respect for elders, the long greetings in the street? We should retain them because they ease the pressures of living considerably. Man, being a social animal, thrives best in the type of social setting that exists in Nigeria. Extreme individualism only generates despair and antisocial behaviour instanced by the senseless murders we read of in Western countries, where a man may shoot people for fun or publicity. Such a psychopath represents man at the lowest possible level of existence, whatever material comforts he may surround himself with.

There is one more reason why we should not throw overboard our cherished social graces, no matter what the pressures of modern living may be. It is that life is more real, has more meaning, when we interact very closely with other human beings. Philosophers who argue that reality does not exist are not mad; they merely emphasize the fact that we have to persuade ourselves continually that we are real and that the outside world is real also. Linking hands with another human being provides that persuasion in a way that nothing else does.

References

INTRODUCTION

1 A. Talbot, *Some Nigerian Fertility Cults* (London and New York, 1967), p. 84.
2 ibid., p. 65.
3 C. K. Meek, *The Northern Tribes of Nigeria* (London, 1971), vol. I, p. 25.
4 A. G. Leonard, *The Lower Niger and its Tribes* (London, 1968), p. 495.
5 C. L. Temple, *Notes on the Tribes of Northern Nigeria* (London, 1965), preface.

CHAPTER 1: RELIGION

1 B. Russell, 'Why I am not a Christian', in *Nobel Prize Library* (New York, 1971), p. 276.
2 ibid., p. 268.
3 St Augustine, 'City of God', in A. I. Melden (ed.), *Ethical Theories* (Englewood Cliffs, N.J., 1967), p. 169.
4 ibid., p. 196.
5 B. Idowu, *Olodumare* (London, 1977), p. 146.
6 B. Russell, *Human Society in Ethics and Politics* (London, 1954), p. 27.
7 *Exodus* XX: 1–3.
8 *The Book of Mormon* (Salt Lake City, 1973), introduction.
9 W. Abimbola, *Ifa* (Ibadan, 1976), p. 51.
10 St Augustine, 'City of God', p. 173.
11 Temple, *Notes on the Tribes of Northern Nigeria*, p. 99.
12 ibid., p. 105.
13 A. Oguntiyi, *History of Ekiti*, p. 35.
14 Leonard, *The Lower Niger and its Tribes*, p. 208.
15 J. Mbiti, *African Religions and Philosophy* (London, 1977), p. 165.
16 Meek, *The Northern Tribes of Nigeria*, vol. II, p. 35.
17 ibid., p. 38.
18 Idowu, *Olodumare*, p. 211.
19 E. Ilogu, *Christianity and Igbo Culture* (Lagos and New York, 1974), p. 41.

CHAPTER 2: SECRET SOCIETIES

1 N. A. Fadipe, *The Sociology of the Yoruba* (Ibadan, 1970), p. 245.
2 ibid.
3 ibid., p. 248.

4 ibid.
5 E. O. Bassey, 'Secret Societies in South Eastern State', in *Heritage*, no. 1, undated (Calabar, Nigeria, c.1974), p. 36.
6 ibid., p. 37.
7 ibid.
8 Ilogu, *Christianity and Igbo Culture*, p. 16.
9 Meek, *The Northern Tribes of Nigeria*, vol. II, p. 93.
10 Temple, *Notes on the Tribes of Northern Nigeria*, p. 184.
11 ibid., p. 367.
12 Nwankwo Ezeabasili, 'Should Social Clubs Be Banned?', in *Weekly Star*, Enugu, 22 July 1979.

CHAPTER 3: MURDER, THEFT AND ADULTERY

1 Temple, *Notes on the Tribes of Northern Nigeria*, p. 220.
2 A. Talbot, *The Peoples of Southern Nigeria*, vol. III (London, 1969), p. 637.
3 ibid., p. 670
4 Temple, *Notes on the Tribes of Northern Nigeria*, p. 42.
5 Talbot, *The Peoples of Southern Nigeria*, vol. III, p. 650.
6 ibid., p. 642.
7 ibid., p. 645.
8 Temple, *Notes on the Tribes of Northern Nigeria*, p. 93.
9 ibid., p. 112.
10 Talbot, *The Peoples of Southern Nigeria*, vol. III, p. 658.
11 ibid., p. 656.
12 Temple, *Notes on the Tribes of Northern Nigeria*, p. 103.
13 ibid., p. 179.
14 Talbot., *The Peoples of Southern Nigeria*, vol. III, p. 653.
15 ibid., p. 638.
16 Temple, *Notes on the Tribes of Northern Nigeria*, p. 321.
17 ibid., p. 168.
18 Talbot, *The Peoples of Southern Nigeria*, vol. III, pp. 645–62.
19 Temple, *Notes on the Tribes of Northern Nigeria*, p. 151.
20 ibid., p. 168.
21 Talbot, *The Peoples of Southern Nigeria*, vol. III, p. 649.
22 ibid., table 19.
23 ibid., p. 664.
24 ibid., p. 672.
25 ibid., p. 643.
26 Temple, *Notes on the Tribes of Northern Nigeria*, p. 64.
27 Talbot, *The Peoples of Southern Nigeria*, vol. III, p. 635.
28 ibid., p. 673.
29 ibid., table 19.
30 ibid., p. 636.
31 Temple, *Notes on the Tribes of Northern Nigeria*, p. 321.
32 ibid., p. 125.
33 ibid., p. 256.

34 ibid., p. 359.
35 Talbot, *The Peoples of Southern Nigeria*, vol. III, p. 661.
36 ibid., table 19.
37 ibid., pp. 631, 650.
38 Temple, *Notes on the Tribes of Northern Nigeria*, p. 81.
39 Meek, *The Northern Tribes of Nigeria*, vol. I, p. 276.
40 Talbot, *The Peoples of Southern Nigeria*, vol. III, table 19.
41 ibid.
42 ibid.
43 Temple, *Notes on the Tribes of Northern Nigeria*, p. 73.
44 Talbot, *The Peoples of Southern Nigeria*, vol. III, pp. 654–62.
45 ibid., table 19.
46 ibid.
47 ibid.
48 ibid.
49 ibid.
50 Temple, *Notes on the Tribes of Northern Nigeria*, p. 241.
51 ibid., pp. 52, 151.
52 Talbot, *The Peoples of Southern Nigeria*, vol. III, pp. 635, 639.
53 Temple, *Notes on the Tribes of Northern Nigeria*, p. 242.
54 ibid., p. 244.
55 ibid., p. 287.
56 ibid., p. 151.
57 T. O. Elias, *Law in a Developing Society* (Benin, 1973), p. 37.

CHAPTER 4: SUPERNATURAL CRIMES

1   Talbot, *The Peoples of Southern Nigeria*, vol. II, p. 206.
2   ibid., p. 208.
3   Temple, *Notes on the Tribes of Northern Nigeria*, p. 168.
4   ibid., p. 315.
5   Talbot, *The Peoples of Southern Nigeria*, vol. II, p. 209.
6   ibid., p. 210.
7   C. K. Meek, *A Sudanese Kingdom* (New York, 1969), p. 301.
8   S. F. Nadel, *A Black Byzantium* (London, 1942), p. 148.
9   *Drum* magazine, September 1979, pp. 7–9.
10 ibid.
11 'Witchcraft', in *The American People's Encyclopedia*, vol. 19 (New York, 1962), p. 807.
12 Temple, *Notes on the Tribes of Northern Nigeria*, p. 237.
13 Talbot, *The Peoples of Southern Nigeria*, vol. III, p. 713.
14 ibid., pp. 716–19.
15 ibid., table 22.
16 ibid., p. 717.
17 Temple, *Notes on the Tribes of Northern Nigeria*, p. 145.
18 E. Ilogu, 'The Problem of Christian Ethics among the Igbo of Nigeria', in *Ikenga*, vol. 3, nos. 1 and 2, p. 41.

CHAPTER 5: WARFARE

1   G. T. Basden, *Among the Ibos of Nigeria* (London, 1966), p. 202.
2   J. F. Ajayi and Robert Smith, *Yoruba Warfare in the 19th Century* (Ibadan and London, 1964), p. 9.
3   Charles Orr, *The Making of Northern Nigeria* (London, 1965), p. 125.
4   Laura Bohannan and Paul Bohannan, *The Tiv of Central Nigeria* (London, 1969), p. 13.
5   Talbot, *The Peoples of Southern Nigeria*, vol. I, p. 177.
6   M. Crowder, *The Story of Nigeria* (London, 1978), p. 164.
7   Shehu Shagari and Jean Boyd, *Uthman Dan Fodio* (Lagos, 1978), p. x.
8   Crowder, *The Story of Nigeria*, p. 75.
9   S. I. Bosah, *Groundwork of the History and Culture of Onitsha* (Onitsha, c.1979), pp. 3–4.
10 Quoted by G. G. Robinson in his report on the inquiry into the Okrika-Kalabari dispute, March 1950, p. 1.
11 ibid., p. 2.
12 ibid., p. 5.
13 Talbot, *The Peoples of Southern Nigeria*, vol. III, p. 821.
14 ibid., p. 838.
15 ibid., p. 835.
16 ibid., p. 823.
17 Nadel, *A Black Byzantium*, p. 110.
18 Temple, *Notes on the Tribes of Northern Nigeria*, p. 262.
19 Bohannan and Bohannan, *The Tiv of Central Nigeria*, p. 25.
20 'Cannibalism', in *The American People's Encyclopedia*, vol. 4 (New York, 1962), p. 680.
21 'Donner Party', in ibid.
22 P. Read, *Alive* (London, 1973), p. 269.
23 Talbot, *The Peoples of Southern Nigeria*, vol. III, table 26.
24 ibid.
25 Temple, *Notes on the Tribes of Northern Nigeria*, p. 329.
26 A. Oyebola, *Black Man's Dilemma* (Lagos, 1976), p. 9.

CHAPTER 6: SLAVERY

1   W. Rodney, 'West Africa and the Atlantic Slave Trade', Historical Association of Tanzania, Paper No. 2, p. 10.
2   Talbot, *The Peoples of Southern Nigeria*, vol. III, p. 695.
3   Crowder, *The Story of Nigeria*, p. 65.
4   F. D. Lugard, *Reports on the Amalgamation of Nigeria*, compiled by A. H. M. Kirk-Green (London, 1968), p. 120.
5   Fadipe, *The Sociology of the Yoruba*, p. 182.
6   ibid., p. 186.
7   Talbot, *The Peoples of Southern Nigeria*, vol. III, p. 699.
8   V. C. Uchendu, *The Igbo of Southeast Nigeria* (New York, 1965), p. 88.
9   K. K. Nair, *Politics and Society in Southeastern Nigeria* (London, 1972), p. 48.

10   Meek, *The Northern Tribes of Nigeria*, vol. I, p. 289.
11   ibid., p. 290.
12   Meek, *A Sudanese Kingdom*, p. 174.
13   *Genesis* XVI.
14   Russell, *Human Society in Ethics and Politics*, p. 104.
15   Nadel, *A Black Byzantium*, p. 103.

CHAPTER 7: CONCEPTS OF GOODNESS

1   Aristotle, *Nichomachean Ethics*, transl. H. Rackham (Cambridge, Mass.,),
     p. 3.
2   G. E. Moore, *Principia Ethica* (Cambridge, 1976), p. 6.
3   J. Bentham, 'Principles of Morals and Legislation', in *British Moralists*
     (Oxford, 1969), p. 974.
4   I. Kant, *The Metaphysics of Ethics*, transl. T. K. Abbott, (London, 1923),
     p. 10.
5   Russell, *Human Society in Ethics and Politics*, p. 80.
6   Idowu, *Olodumare*, p. 146.
7   S. Johnson, *The History of the Yorubas* (Lagos, 1973), p. 101.
8   J. A. Sofola, *African Culture and the African Personality* (Ibadan, 1973), ch. 4.
9   A. Ojo, *Yoruba Culture* (Ife and London, 1966), p. 134.
10   ibid., p. 134.
11   *Guinness Book of Records* (Enfield, Middx, 1971 edn.).
12   G. T. Basden, *Niger Ibos* (London, 1966), p. 381.
13   Shagari and Boyd, *Uthman Dan Fodio*, p. x.

CHAPTER 8: SOCIAL DISCRIMINATION

1   Ilogu, *Christianity and Igbo Culture*, p. 72.
2   A. Talbot, *Tribes of the Niger Delta* (London, 1967), p. 301.

CHAPTER 9: SEXUAL DISCRIMINATION

1   *Newsweek*, 18 February 1980, p. 30.
2   ibid.
3   I. Nzimiro, *Studies in Ibo Political Systems* (London, 1972), p. 138.
4   Meek, *The Northern Tribes of Nigeria*, vol. I, p. 155.
5   C. Ifeka-Moller, 'Female Militancy and Colonial Revolt', in *Perceiving
     Women* (London, 1977), p. 132.
6   H. A. Gailey, *The Road to Aba* (London, 1971), p. 7.
7   Temple, *Notes on the Tribes of Northern Nigeria*, p. 131.
8   Talbot, *The Peoples of Southern Nigeria*, vol. III, p. 428.
9   Meek, *A Sudanese Kingdom*, pp. 340–1.
10   Nadel, *A Black Byzantium*, p. 147.

116 REFERENCES

11 M. Mead, 'Male and Female', in *The Measure of Mankind* (New York, 1963), p. 57.
12 J. O. Akande, *Laws and Customs Affecting Women's Status in Nigeria* (Lagos, 1979), p. 9.

CHAPTER 10: *AWUF*

1 Nzimiro, *Studies in Ibo Political Systems*, p. 121.
2 Talbot, *The Peoples of Southern Nigeria*, vol. III, p. 620.
3 Fadipe, *The Sociology of the Yoruba*, p. 321.
4 Crowder, *The Story of Nigeria*, p. 73.
5 Nadel, *A Black Byzantium*, p. 166.
6 Temple, *Notes on the Tribes of Northern Nigeria*, p. 304.
7 Talbot, *The Peoples of Southern Nigeria*, vol. III, p. 622.
8 Meek, *A Sudanese Kingdom*, p. 351.
9 Writer's observation in Hungary in 1977.

CHAPTER 11: LEADERSHIP

1 Uchendu, *The Igbo of Southeast Nigeria*, p. 90.
2 Basden, *Niger Ibos*, p. 132.
3 Nzimiro, *Studies in Ibo Political Systems*, preface.
4 Ilogu, *Christianity and Igbo Culture*, p. 31.
5 Talbot, *The Peoples of Southern Nigeria*, vol. III, p. 591.
6 ibid., p. 592.
7 Crowder, *The Story of Nigeria*, p. 45.
8 Johnson, *The History of the Yorubas*, p. 40.
9 Ojo, *Yoruba Culture*, p. 38.
10 ibid., p. 156.
11 Nzimiro, *Studies in Ibo Political Systems*, p. 32.
12 Meek, *A Sudanese Kingdom*, p. 334.
13 ibid., p. 333.

Bibliography

Abimbola, W., *Ifa* (Ibadan, 1976).

Ajayi, J. F. and Smith, R., *Yoruba Warfare in the 19th Century* (Ibadan and London, 1964).

Aristotle, *Nichomachean Ethics*, transl. H. Rackham (Cambridge, Mass.).

Basden, G. T., *Among the Ibos of Nigeria* (London, 1966).

Basden, G. T., *Niger Ibos* (London, 1966).

Bohannan, L., and Bohannan, P., *The Tiv of Central Nigeria* (London, 1969).

Bosah, S. I., *Groundwork of the History and Culture of Onitsha* (Onitsha, undated c.1979).

Crowder, M., *The Story of Nigeria* (London, 1978).

Elias, T. O., *Law in a Developing Society* (Benin, 1973).

Fadipe, N. A., *The Sociology of the Yoruba* (Ibadan, 1970).

Idowu, B., *Olodumare* (London, 1977).

Ilogu, E., *Christianity and Igbo Culture* (Lagos and New York, 1974).

Johnson, S., *The History of the Yorubas* (Lagos, 1973).

Kant, I., *The Metaphysics of Ethics*, transl. T. K. Abbott (London, 1923).

Leonard, A. G., *The Lower Niger and its Tribes* (London, 1968).

Lugard, F. D., *Reports on the Amalgamation of Nigeria*, compiled by A. H. M. Kirk-Green (London, 1968).

Mbiti, J., *African Religions and Philosophy* (London, 1977).

Meek, C. K., *A Sudanese Kingdom* (New York, 1969).

Meek, C. K., *The Northern Tribes of Nigeria*, 2 vols. (London, 1971).

Melden, A. I. (ed.), *Ethical Theories* (Englewood Cliffs, N.J., 1967).

Moore, G. E., *Principia Ethica* (Cambridge, 1976).

Nadel, S. F., *A Black Byzantium* (London, 1942).

Nair, K. K., *Politics and Society in Southeastern Nigeria* (London, 1972).

Nzimiro, I., *Studies in Ibo Political Systems* (London, 1972).

Oguntuyi, A., *itan Ado-Ekiti/A History of Ado-Ekiti* (Akure, 194?).

Ojo, A., *Yoruba Culture* (Ife and London, 1966).

Orr, C., *The Making of Northern Nigeria* (London, 1965).

Oyebola, A., *Black Man's Dilemma* (Lagos, 1976).

Read, P., *Alive* (London, 1973).

Russell, B., 'Why I am not a Christian', in *Nobel Prize Library* (New York, 1971).

Russell, B., *Human Society in Ethics and Politics* (London, 1954).

Shagari, S., and Boyd, J., *Uthman Dan Fodio* (Lagos, 1978).

Talbot, A., *Tribes of the Niger Delta* (London, 1967).

Talbot, A., *Some Nigerian Fertility Cults* (London and New York, 1967).

Talbot, A., *The Peoples of Southern Nigeria*, 4 vols. (London, 1969).

Temple, C. L., *Notes on the Tribes of Northern Nigeria* (London, 1965).

Uchendu, V. C., *The Igbo of Southeast Nigeria* (New York, 1965).

Index

Abam, 35, 47
Aba Women's War, 73
Abiku, 5
Abomination, 28
Abua, 15, 27
Aburi, 30
Adultery, 17–19
Afikpo, 16
Age groups, 13
Ajayi and Smith, 32
Ajibola, J. O., viii
Akande, J. O., 77
Akpan, Edet Edem, 24
Alafin of Oyo, 34
Aluu, 43
Amadioha, 4, 78
Amina, Queen of Zaria, 73
Ancestors, 7
Angas, 6
Anglican church, 78
Aquinas, St. Thomas, 3
Arago, 15, 17
Arochukwu, 11
Aro, 17, 33, 44
Aristotle, 50
Augustine, St., 3, 4
Awka, 17, 35
Awuf, 82–93
  influence of religion, 87, 93
  in the civil service, 88
  in politics, 89
  and Nigerian intellectuals, 92
  and students, 92
  and living standard, 92

and communism, 93

Babylonians, 48
Bakundu, 18
Basden, G. T., 30, 64, 96
Bassa, 15, 17
Batta, 18
Bentham, Jeremy, 51
Bende, 11
Benin:
  art treasures, 33, 49
  massacre, 32
  mercenaries, 35
Berkeley, 2
Berom, 5
Biafrans, 39
Bible, 4
Blackman's Dilemma (A. Oyebola), 40
Bloodmen, 46
Boki, 18
Bolewa, 17
Bonny, 34, 44, 46
Book of Mormon, 4
Bornu, 33, 47
Bosah, S. I., 33
Brass, 24
Britain, 37
Burial, 9, 64
Burra, 15, 18

Calabar, 49
Cannibalism, 37
Catholic church, 37, 68, 78
Chamba, 5, 18
China, 37
Christian religion, 4, 6
Christians, 68
Chukwu, 4, 44, 45, 68,

78, 97 (*see also* Long Juju)
Civilisation, 40
Civil service, 88
Civil War, Nigerian, 39, 70, 93
Code of conduct, 89
Contentment, 55
Criminal code, 20
Criminals, 43
Crowder, Michael, 33, 45, 86

Dahomi, 32
Dakaru, 35
Dakkakarri, 15
Death penalty, 15–16
Degema, 46
Delta household, vii
Dependents, 106 (*see also* Extended family)
Discrimination, social, 65–70
  racial, 66
  religious, 67, 68, 78
  status, 69
  ideological, 69
  political, 69
Dodo secret society, 12
Donner Party, 37
Dracula, 21
Dukawa, 5

Earth goddess, 27, 46
Eddah, 28
Edo, 15, 19, 27, 33
Education, 80
Efik, 39, 46
Effiong, Lt-Col, Phillip, 39